The Old Farmer's ALMANAC for Kids

VOLUME 2

YANKEE PUBLISHING
INCORPORATED

***The Old Farmer's Almanac* Books**

Group publisher: John Pierce
Publisher: Sherin Wight

Series editor: Janice Stillman
Art director: Margo Letourneau
Copy editor: Jack Burnett
Contributors: Alice Cary, Laurie Goldman, Mare-Anne Jarvela, L. Patricia Kite, Stacey Kusterbeck, Celeste Longacre, Martie Majoros, Sarah Perreault, Heidi Stonehill
Indexer: Lida Stinchfield

Production director: Susan Gross
Production manager: David Ziarnowski
Production artists: Lucille Rines, Rachel Kipka, Janet Calhoun, Sarah Heineke

Companion Web site: Almanac4kids.com
Web site editor: Mare-Anne Jarvela
Activity guide writer: Faith Brynie
Design coordinator: Lisa Traffie
Programmer: Peter Rukavina

For additional information about this and other publications from *The Old Farmer's Almanac,* visit **Almanac.com** or call **1-800-ALMANAC**

Distributed in the book trade in the United States by Houghton Mifflin and in Canada by H.B. Fenn.

Direct-to-retail and bulk sales are handled by Cindy Schlosser, 800-729-9265, ext. 126, or Stacey Korpi, ext. 160

Yankee Publishing Inc., P.O. Box 520, 1121 Main Street, Dublin, New Hampshire 03444

ISBN-13: 978-1-57198-434-0

FIRST PRINTING OF VOLUME 2

Thank you for buying this Almanac! Thanks, too, to everyone who had a hand in producing it and getting it to market, including printers, distributors, and sales and delivery people.

PRINTED IN THE UNITED STATES OF AMERICA

Dear Kids (and Kids at Heart),

Life was a lot simpler in 1766. That was the year in which Robert B. Thomas was born on a farm in Grafton, Massachusetts. Back then, television and telephones, cars and computers didn't exist. People didn't even have electricity!

But Robert B. found all kinds of ways to have fun. He probably looked into the sky to find the stars and planets, tended a garden of fruits and vegetables, played sports, did a few magic tricks, found bait to go fishing, wondered why spiders spin webs and how ants know when rain is coming, hunted toads, saved his stuff in a time capsule, made ice cream and birdhouses, watched as sheep's fleece was turned into a sweater, rode horses, picked apples, and more.

Just like Robert B., kids today like to learn, to figure things out, to try new ways of doing things, to explore, to laugh, and to discover. When Robert B. grew up, he founded *The Old Farmer's Almanac* (a new edition is still printed every year!). This kids' edition is dedicated to him and to kids of all ages because even though times change, kids don't. Kids still want to have fun.

We hope you enjoy this Almanac. Let us know what you like (and don't like) at **Almanac4kids.com/tellus** or send a letter to *The Old Farmer's Almanac for Kids*, P.O. Box 520, Dublin, NH 03444.

Thanks!

Contents

CALENDAR

Calendar Pages 8
Almanac Oddities 20

ASTRONOMY

The Reason for the Seasons . . 24
Party Time 26
A Month of Moons. 29
Famous Unknowns 30
Perplexing Pluto 33
Saturn: The *Real* Lord of the Rings 34

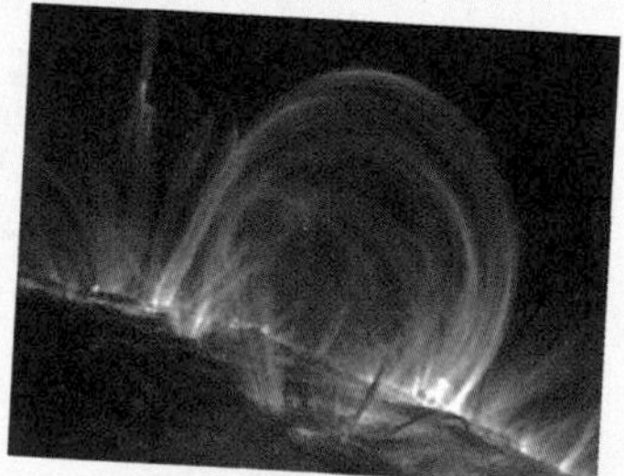

10 Burning Facts About the Sun 36
I Wish I May, I Wish I Might Find My Own Meteorite! . . 41
Star Art 42

GARDENING

The Most Unloved Flower . . . 46
A Gardener's Worst Fears . . . 49

A Prickly Subject 50
Beans, Bountiful Beans! 52
Grow a Vegetable Forest 56
An Earful About Corn 59
Whoopee! It's Watermelon Time! 60
Eat Dirt? Yecchh! 62

ON THE FARM

Hey, Ewe! 64

Hooray for Horses! 68
Fowl Matters 73
A Is for Apple. 74
Is It a Fruit or a Vegetable? . . 77

WEATHER

Weather Wizards. 78
Beware of Black Blizzards . . . 82
Food Floods!. 86
Weather Phobias. 89

The World's Fuzziest Forecaster 90

Looking for Something to Do?

You'll find scores of fun things to do in our **ACTIVITY GUIDE** at **Almanac4kids.com/guide.**

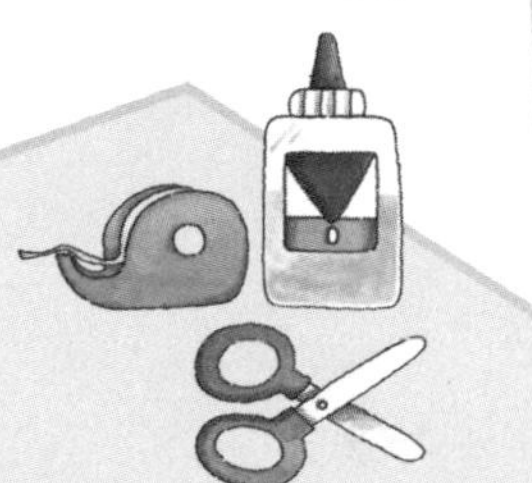

NATURE

By the Sea, By the Sea, By the Beautiful Sea 92
Make a Gourd Birdhouse . . . 96
Creepy, Crawly, Coming at You! 98

continued on next page

Contents (continued)

Going Batty. 102
Toad-ily Awesome. 106
Meet the Winter Warriors . . 108
Tracker's Guide 111

HISTORY

The Shortcut That Wasn't . . 112

The First Great Gold Rush. . 116
The Color of Money 119
Three Little Bears. 120
The Scoop on Ice Cream Through the Ages. 124

AMUSEMENT

Right On, Left-Handers! . . . 130
Mind Manglers 133

Astrology for Pets. 134
Hocus-Pocus! 136
Jumping for Joy. 140

SPORTS

Ben Franklin: Statesman . . . Scientist . . . Swimmer? . . . 144
The Game Game 147
Got Bait? 148
Baseball: Get a Grip! 151

You Go, Girl! 152

Ride 'Em, Cowboy! 154

Two-Wheeling Through Time 158

HEALTH

In With the Good Air, Out With the Bad 164

For Crying Out Loud 168

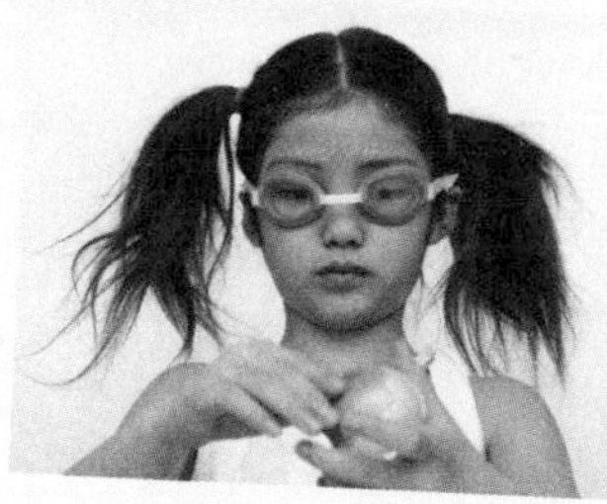

You Are Getting Sleepy, Ver-r-r-y Sleepy 170

Know Why George Washington Never Smiled? 174

Warts Away! 177

Read Something—and Do Something!

For almost every Almanac article, there is a great **ACTIVITY** or **PROJECT** at **Almanac4kids.com/guide.**

USEFUL THINGS

Mayonnaise Magic 178

Save Your Stuff! 180

Where Do You Fit in Your Family Tree? 183

Your Body Rules 184

Tied Up in Knots 185

Home Cooking 186

Answers to Mind Manglers . . 187

Acknowledgments 188

Index 190

January

THE FIRST MONTH

JANUARY HATH 31 DAYS

1	**New Year's Day** • Patriot Paul Revere born, 1735
2	*From small beginnings come great things.*
3	George Washington defeated British in Battle of Princeton, N.J., 1777
4	Jacob of Brothers Grimm born, 1785
5	**Twelfth Night** • Babe Ruth sold to New York Yankees, 1920
6	**Epiphany** • Albany became the capital of N.Y., 1797
7	Galileo discovered first three moons of Jupiter, 1610
8	Lewis and Clark saw whale bones, 1806
9	Citrus freeze in southern California, 1888
10	Singer Rod Stewart born, 1945
11	First disco opened, Los Angeles, 1963
12	Statesman John Hancock born, 1737
13	Opera heard live for first time on radio, 1910
14	Blizzard hit Chicago, 1918
15	Civil rights leader Martin Luther King Jr. born, 1929
16	*Trust the man who sings in his bathtub.*
17	Statesman Benjamin Franklin born, 1706 • Pres. R. Hayes died, 1893
18	–54°F in Embarrass, Minn., 2005
19	Temperature dropped 50 degrees in Portsmouth, N.H., 1810
20	"Kennedy Inaugural Storm" hit East Coast, 1961
21	*To question a wise man is the beginning of wisdom.*
22	President Lyndon B. Johnson died, 1973
23	Willie Mays elected to Baseball Hall of Fame, 1979
24	Moving picture of solar eclipse taken from dirigible, 1925
25	Musician Alicia Keys born, 1981
26	*Fog in January brings a wet spring.*
27	Western Union sent its last telegram, 2006
28	U.S. Coast Guard established, 1915
29	Winds up to 113 mph in North Head, Wash., 1921
30	**Raccoons mate now.** • Yerba Buena renamed San Francisco, 1847
31	*Little strokes fell great oaks.* –Benjamin Franklin

February

THE SECOND MONTH

FEB. HATH 28 OR 29 DAYS

1	First dental college incorporated, Md., 1840
2	**Candlemas • Groundhog Day**
3	*When life gives you scraps, make quilts.*
4	Ice storm hit Mass., N.H., and Maine, 1959
5	Walt Disney's *Peter Pan* premiered, 1953
6	President Dwight D. Eisenhower shot a hole-in-one, 1968
7	Manufacturer John Deere born, 1804
8	The Boy Scouts of America incorporated, 1910
9	First flight of a Boeing 727 aircraft, 1963
10	New Delhi became the capital of India, 1931
11	*I Love Lucy* won Emmy for Best Situation Comedy, 1954
12	Pres. Abraham Lincoln born, 1809 • Snow in Fort Myers, Fla., 1977
13	First Lady Bess Truman born, 1885
14	**Valentine's Day** • Dolly, the cloned sheep, died, 2003
15	Reformer Susan B. Anthony born, 1820
16	**Winter's back breaks.** • Ventriloquist Edgar Bergen born, 1903
17	National Congress of Mothers, later known as PTA, founded, 1897
18	Elm Farm Ollie became first cow to fly in an airplane, 1930
19	Actress Haylie Duff born, 1985
20	An auto-airplane combination, Arrowbile, completed for testing, 1937
21	Dedication of Washington Monument, 1885
22	Pres. George Washington born, 1732 • Fistfight in U.S. Senate, 1902
23	Liberty Bell developed final, irreparable crack, 1846
24	Thomas Edison married Mina Miller, 1886
25	*February makes a bridge and March breaks it.*
26	*Spelling Bee,* the first quiz show, aired on television, 1940
27	First Mardi Gras celebration in New Orleans, 1827
28	Kentucky Derby winning horse Smarty Jones born, 2001
29	**Leap Day** • *He who leaps high must take a long run.*

March

THE THIRD MONTH

MARCH HATH 31 DAYS

1	*Better to give a penny than lend twenty.*
2	World premiere of the original *King Kong* movie, 1933
3	Anne Sullivan began teaching deaf/blind Helen Keller, 1887
4	*Every man knows best where his own shoe pinches.*
5	Boston Massacre, five American rioters killed, 1770
6	16 tornadoes in Ill. and Ind., 1961
7	World's first jazz recording released, 1917
8	Wheeled suitcase with collapsible towing handle patented, 1994
9	First animal returned from space, a dog, aboard *Sputnik 9,* 1961
10	Thomas Jefferson became U.S. minister to France, 1785
11	First public basketball game played, Springfield, Mass., 1892
12	Girl Scouts started, 1912 • Musician James Taylor born, 1948
13	Harvard University renamed for clergyman John Harvard, 1639
14	President Warren Harding filed income tax, 1923
15	**Beware the ides of March.** • Rainmaker hired by N.Y.C., 1950
16	First American visited Russian space station *Mir,* 1995
17	**St. Patrick** • British forces evacuated Boston, 1776
18	Comedian Dane Cook born, 1972
19	Explorer David Livingstone born, 1813
20	Physicist Sir Isaac Newton died, 1727
21	*In spring, no one thinks of the snow that fell last year.*
22	E. G. Otis installed first passenger elevator, 1857
23	Edmonton, Alta., reached a toasty 72°F, 1889
24	Singer Elvis Presley inducted into army, 1958
25	First U.S. public demonstration of pancake making, N.Y.C., 1882
26	Poet Walt Whitman died, 1892
27	Actress Brenda Song born, 1988
28	*Truth and oil always come to the top.*
29	Vesta, brightest asteroid, discovered, 1807
30	Official opening of Canada's first subway, in Toronto, 1954
31	Daylight Saving Time observed for first time in U.S., 1918

April

THE FOURTH MONTH

APRIL HATH 30 DAYS

1	**All Fools'** • In France, today is *Poisson d'Avril,* April Fish.
2	U.S. Mint established, 1792 • Blizzard in Chicago, 1975
3	The Pony Express began postal service, 1860
4	President W. H. Harrison died, a month after his inauguration, 1841
5	Pocahontas married Englishman John Rolfe, 1614
6	U.S. declared war on Germany and entered World War I, 1917
7	*The fiddle makes the feast.* • Actor Jackie Chan born, 1954
8	The League of Nations assembled for last time, Geneva, Switz., 1946
9	Houston Astrodome hosted its first baseball game, 1965
10	*Plough deep and you will have plenty of corn.*
11	First Easter egg roll at the White House, 1878
12	Dr. Peter Safar, originator of CPR, born, 1924
13	President Thomas Jefferson born, 1743
14	*Titanic* struck iceberg in North Atlantic, 1912
15	Last day U.S. silver coins allowed to circulate in Canada, 1870
16	Sharpshooter Annie Oakley hit 100 clay targets in a row, 1922
17	Actress Jennifer Garner born, 1972
18	Strong earthquake hit San Francisco, 1906
19	Canadian John C. Miles won Boston Marathon, 1926
20	Vice President George Clinton died in office, 1812
21	*David Dows,* largest five-masted schooner of its time, launched, 1881
22	First European tour by U.S. orchestra began, 1920
23	Hank Aaron hit his first major league home run, 1954
24	*The Old Farmer's Almanac* founder Robert B. Thomas born, 1766
25	N.Y. became first state to require auto license plates, 1901
26	First international satellite, *Ariel 1,* launched, 1962
27	Arbor Day founder Julius Sterling Morton died, 1902
28	Ethel Catherwood, 1928 Olympic gold medal high jumper, born, 1909
29	Weather device TOTO hit by weak tornado in Okla., 1984
30	Franklin D. Roosevelt first president to appear on television, 1939

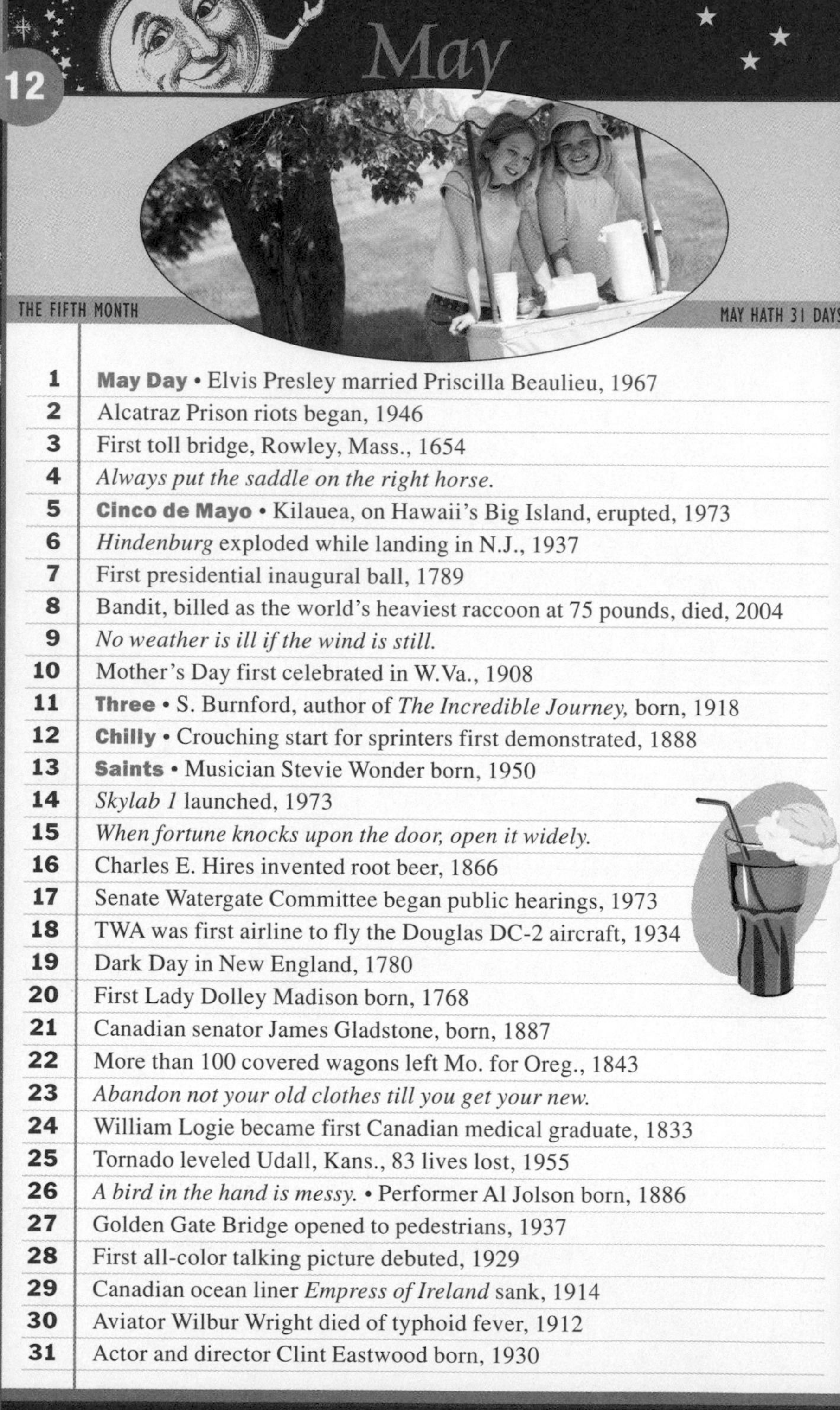

May

THE FIFTH MONTH

MAY HATH 31 DAYS

1	**May Day** • Elvis Presley married Priscilla Beaulieu, 1967
2	Alcatraz Prison riots began, 1946
3	First toll bridge, Rowley, Mass., 1654
4	*Always put the saddle on the right horse.*
5	**Cinco de Mayo** • Kilauea, on Hawaii's Big Island, erupted, 1973
6	*Hindenburg* exploded while landing in N.J., 1937
7	First presidential inaugural ball, 1789
8	Bandit, billed as the world's heaviest raccoon at 75 pounds, died, 2004
9	*No weather is ill if the wind is still.*
10	Mother's Day first celebrated in W.Va., 1908
11	**Three** • S. Burnford, author of *The Incredible Journey,* born, 1918
12	**Chilly** • Crouching start for sprinters first demonstrated, 1888
13	**Saints** • Musician Stevie Wonder born, 1950
14	*Skylab 1* launched, 1973
15	*When fortune knocks upon the door, open it widely.*
16	Charles E. Hires invented root beer, 1866
17	Senate Watergate Committee began public hearings, 1973
18	TWA was first airline to fly the Douglas DC-2 aircraft, 1934
19	Dark Day in New England, 1780
20	First Lady Dolley Madison born, 1768
21	Canadian senator James Gladstone, born, 1887
22	More than 100 covered wagons left Mo. for Oreg., 1843
23	*Abandon not your old clothes till you get your new.*
24	William Logie became first Canadian medical graduate, 1833
25	Tornado leveled Udall, Kans., 83 lives lost, 1955
26	*A bird in the hand is messy.* • Performer Al Jolson born, 1886
27	Golden Gate Bridge opened to pedestrians, 1937
28	First all-color talking picture debuted, 1929
29	Canadian ocean liner *Empress of Ireland* sank, 1914
30	Aviator Wilbur Wright died of typhoid fever, 1912
31	Actor and director Clint Eastwood born, 1930

June

THE SIXTH MONTH — JUNE HATH 30 DAYS

1 Oscar the Grouch's birthday • 39°F, Springfield, Ill., 2003
2 First Lady Martha Washington born, 1731
3 Automobile manufacturer Ransom Eli Olds born, 1864
4 *Even a stopped clock is right twice a day.*
5 Teton Dam in Fremont County, Idaho, broke, 1976
6 First Pa. Horticultural Society exhibition, 1829 • D-Day, 1944
7 Actor Liam Neeson born, 1952
8 Bald Eagle Protection Act passed, 1940

9 Tornado in Worcester County, Mass., 1953
10 Benjamin Franklin's kite-and-key experiment, 1752
11 Phoenix had 1.64 inches of rain, a June record, 1972
12 President George H. W. Bush born, 1924
13 *You can't sell the cow and have the milk.*
14 Strawberries are ripe about now in southern N.H.
15 *Magna Carta* signed, 1215 • Singer Ella Fitzgerald died, 1996
16 Hail, 17 inches in circumference, fell in Dubuque, Iowa, 1882
17 Sir Francis Drake landed on the Pacific Coast, 1579
18 Musician Paul McCartney born, 1942
19 *The ambitious bullfrog puffed and puffed until he burst.*
20 Samuel Morse received patent for telegraph, 1840
21 George Ferris Jr.'s wheel debuted in Chicago, 1893
22 Adolphe Sax patented the saxophone, 1846
23 *Better sense in the head than cents in the pocket.*
24 **Midsummer Day** • Light snow flurries in northern Manitoba, 2005
25 Sitting Bull defeated Gen. George Custer, 1876
26 Opening ceremonies for St. Lawrence Seaway took place, 1959
27 100°F in Fort Yukon, Alaska, 1915
28 King Henry VII born, 1491 • Pres. James Madison died, 1836
29 "Rock Around the Clock" reached the top of the music charts, 1955
30 *Life never stands still: If you don't advance, you recede.*

July

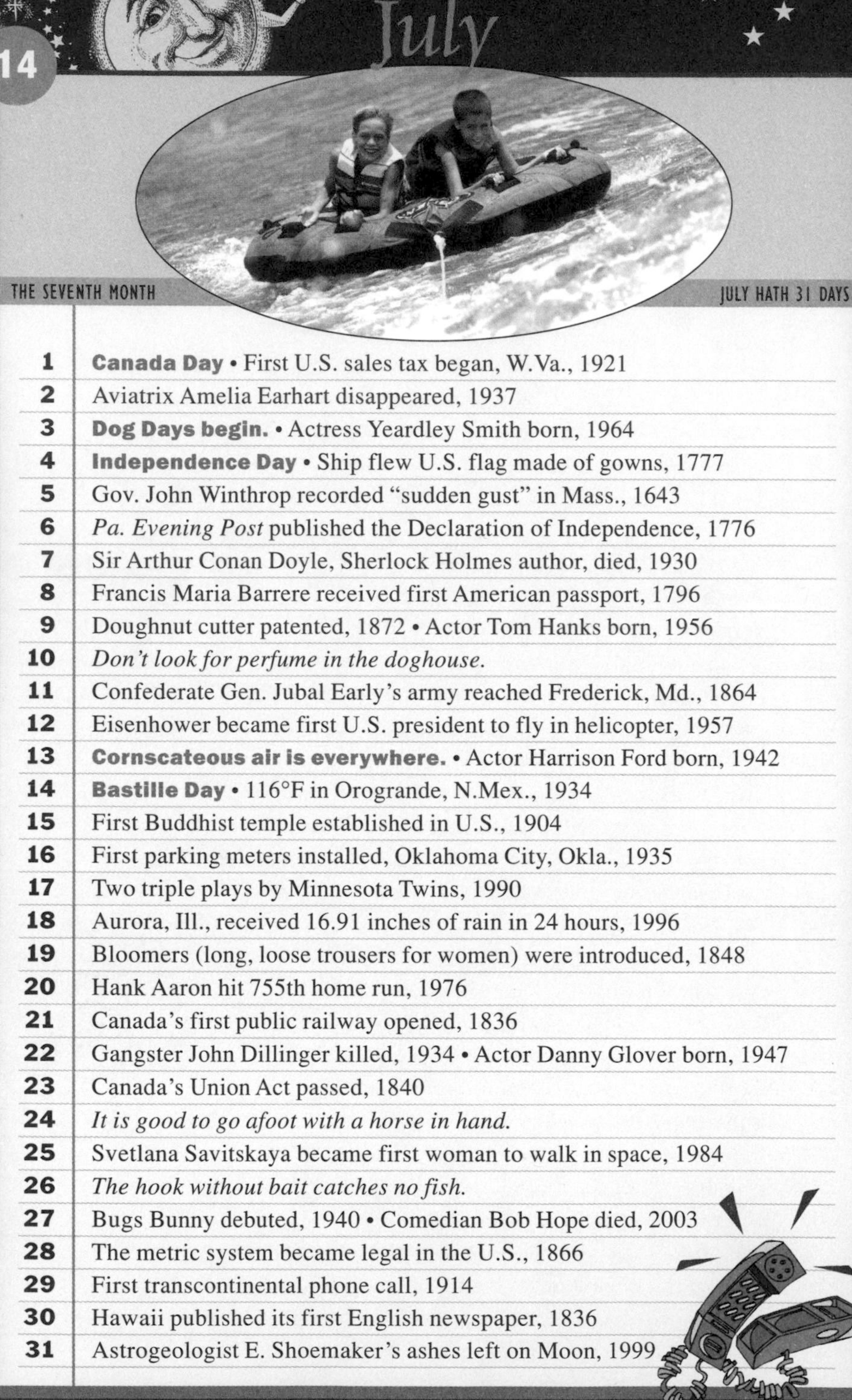

THE SEVENTH MONTH

JULY HATH 31 DAYS

1	**Canada Day** • First U.S. sales tax began, W.Va., 1921
2	Aviatrix Amelia Earhart disappeared, 1937
3	**Dog Days begin.** • Actress Yeardley Smith born, 1964
4	**Independence Day** • Ship flew U.S. flag made of gowns, 1777
5	Gov. John Winthrop recorded "sudden gust" in Mass., 1643
6	*Pa. Evening Post* published the Declaration of Independence, 1776
7	Sir Arthur Conan Doyle, Sherlock Holmes author, died, 1930
8	Francis Maria Barrere received first American passport, 1796
9	Doughnut cutter patented, 1872 • Actor Tom Hanks born, 1956
10	*Don't look for perfume in the doghouse.*
11	Confederate Gen. Jubal Early's army reached Frederick, Md., 1864
12	Eisenhower became first U.S. president to fly in helicopter, 1957
13	**Cornscateous air is everywhere.** • Actor Harrison Ford born, 1942
14	**Bastille Day** • 116°F in Orogrande, N.Mex., 1934
15	First Buddhist temple established in U.S., 1904
16	First parking meters installed, Oklahoma City, Okla., 1935
17	Two triple plays by Minnesota Twins, 1990
18	Aurora, Ill., received 16.91 inches of rain in 24 hours, 1996
19	Bloomers (long, loose trousers for women) were introduced, 1848
20	Hank Aaron hit 755th home run, 1976
21	Canada's first public railway opened, 1836
22	Gangster John Dillinger killed, 1934 • Actor Danny Glover born, 1947
23	Canada's Union Act passed, 1840
24	*It is good to go afoot with a horse in hand.*
25	Svetlana Savitskaya became first woman to walk in space, 1984
26	*The hook without bait catches no fish.*
27	Bugs Bunny debuted, 1940 • Comedian Bob Hope died, 2003
28	The metric system became legal in the U.S., 1866
29	First transcontinental phone call, 1914
30	Hawaii published its first English newspaper, 1836
31	Astrogeologist E. Shoemaker's ashes left on Moon, 1999

August

THE EIGHTH MONTH — AUGUST HATH 31 DAYS

1	**Lammas Day** • Astronomer Helen Hogg born, 1905
2	First street mail boxes installed in U.S., 1858
3	National Basketball Association formed from merger, 1949
4	George Washington became a Master Mason, 1753
5	*When trout refuse bait or fly, there ever is a storm nigh.*
6	Asteroids renamed for *Columbia* crew, 2003
7	Peace Bridge between N.Y. and Ont. opened, 1927
8	*There's more to riding than a pair of boots.*
9	Henry David Thoreau's *Walden* published, 1854
10	First space/Earth wedding, 2003
11	**Dog Days end.** • *Don't keep a dog and bark yourself.*
12	13-year-old diver Marjorie Gestring won Olympic gold medal, 1936
13	Flexible Flyer sled patented, 1889
14	Massive blackout affected parts of North America, 2003
15	Actor Ben Affleck born, 1972
16	Trade between Union and Confederate states prohibited, 1861
17	**Cat Nights commence.** • Hurricane Diane hit N.C., 1955
18	Charles Wilkes began expedition to South Pole, 1838
19	*If you wish another to keep your secret, first keep it yourself.*
20	Salt fell from the sky over Switzerland, 1870
21	Christopher Robin Milne, son of Pooh Bear author, born, 1920
22	Liquid soap patent granted to W. Sheppard, 1865
23	Musical writer Oscar Hammerstein II died, 1960
24	Julie Krone, first female jockey to win a $1 million race, 2003
25	*Asking costs nothing.* • New Orleans founded, 1718
26	Tornado hit train on bridge in Dearborn County, Ind., 1864
27	Missionary Mother Teresa born, 1910
28	First successful U.S. vineyard established, 1798
29	Strange noises heard in sky over London, 1607
30	*Every fish bites sooner or later.* • Boston reached 99°F, 1973
31	Dave Scott became the first person to drive a car on Moon, 1971

September

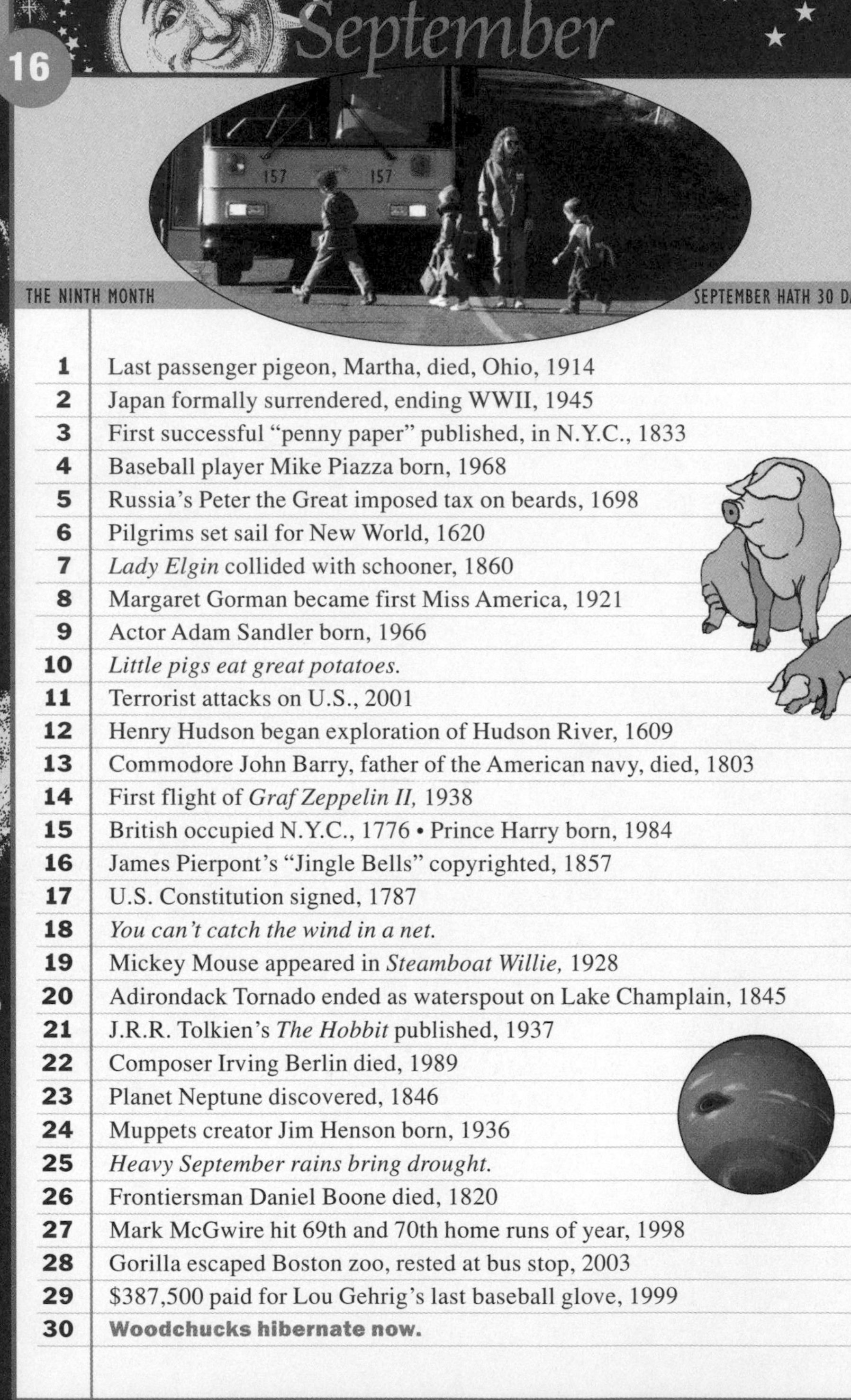

THE NINTH MONTH

SEPTEMBER HATH 30 DAYS

1	Last passenger pigeon, Martha, died, Ohio, 1914
2	Japan formally surrendered, ending WWII, 1945
3	First successful "penny paper" published, in N.Y.C., 1833
4	Baseball player Mike Piazza born, 1968
5	Russia's Peter the Great imposed tax on beards, 1698
6	Pilgrims set sail for New World, 1620
7	*Lady Elgin* collided with schooner, 1860
8	Margaret Gorman became first Miss America, 1921
9	Actor Adam Sandler born, 1966
10	*Little pigs eat great potatoes.*
11	Terrorist attacks on U.S., 2001
12	Henry Hudson began exploration of Hudson River, 1609
13	Commodore John Barry, father of the American navy, died, 1803
14	First flight of *Graf Zeppelin II,* 1938
15	British occupied N.Y.C., 1776 • Prince Harry born, 1984
16	James Pierpont's "Jingle Bells" copyrighted, 1857
17	U.S. Constitution signed, 1787
18	*You can't catch the wind in a net.*
19	Mickey Mouse appeared in *Steamboat Willie,* 1928
20	Adirondack Tornado ended as waterspout on Lake Champlain, 1845
21	J.R.R. Tolkien's *The Hobbit* published, 1937
22	Composer Irving Berlin died, 1989
23	Planet Neptune discovered, 1846
24	Muppets creator Jim Henson born, 1936
25	*Heavy September rains bring drought.*
26	Frontiersman Daniel Boone died, 1820
27	Mark McGwire hit 69th and 70th home runs of year, 1998
28	Gorilla escaped Boston zoo, rested at bus stop, 2003
29	$387,500 paid for Lou Gehrig's last baseball glove, 1999
30	**Woodchucks hibernate now.**

October

THE TENTH MONTH

OCTOBER HATH 31 DAYS

1	Game 1 of first World Series played, 1903
2	*Rest is the sweet sauce of labor.*
3	Pres. Lincoln proclaimed last Thursday in Nov. Thanksgiving, 1863
4	Saxby's Gale caused flooding all over New England, 1869
5	*Better to be the head of a lizard than the tail of a dragon.*
6	A magnitude 2.0 earthquake registered east of Keene, N.H., 2004
7	Cornell University welcomed its first students, 1868
8	Actor Matt Damon born, 1970
9	American Humane Association organized, 1877
10	G. Lorillard introduced tuxedo at ball, Tuxedo Park, N.Y., 1886
11	*Juliana,* first steam-powered ferry in U.S., began service, 1811
12	100-mph winds, Oreg., 1962 • Singer John Denver died, 1997
13	B'nai B'rith founded, 1843
14	Pilot Charles Yeager became first to break sound barrier, 1947
15	Earthquake near Kailua Kona on Big Island of Hawaii, 2006
16	Queen of France Marie Antoinette died, 1793
17	Country musician Alan Jackson born, 1958
18	Russia transferred Alaskan territory to U.S., 1867
19	*Be silent and pass for a philosopher.*
20	Laurel and Hardy's *The Flying Deuces* premiered, 1939
21	Portland, Maine, received 13.32 inches of rain in 24 hours, 1996
22	First recorded solar eclipse, China, 2136 B.C.
23	*Life never gets a goldfish down.* • Bryn Mawr College opened, 1885
24	Schooner *Bluenose* won International Fishermen's Trophy, 1921
25	**Little brown bats hibernate now.**
26	R. Krueger became World Rock Paper Scissors champion, 2003
27	DuPont announced invention of nylon, 1938
28	U.S. police began fingerprinting, 1904
29	First ballpoint pens went on sale at $12.50 apiece, 1945
30	*Every pumpkin is known by its stem.* • Pres. John Adams born, 1735
31	**All Hallows' Eve** • Nev. became 36th state, 1864

November

THE ELEVENTH MONTH

NOVEMBER HATH 30 DAYS

1	**All Saints'** • First national weather service in U.S. began, 1870
2	*To the brave man, every land is a native country.*
3	*Good Morning America* debuted, 1975
4	Sunspot produced record-breaking X40-class solar flare, 2003
5	Baseball player Johnny Damon born, 1973
6	*Who throws a stone at the sky may have it fall on his head.*
7	First Lady Eleanor Roosevelt died, 1962
8	Abraham Lincoln reelected as U.S. president, 1864
9	Berlin Wall came down, 1989
10	U.S. Marine Corps established, 1775
11	**Veterans Day** • Leonardo DiCaprio born, 1974
12	**Indian Summer** • A heavy snowstorm hit New England, 1820
13	Thousands of meteors fell per hour, 1833
14	*You can not make a crab walk straight.*
15	Astronomer Sir William Herschel born, 1738
16	President Nixon approved construction of an Alaskan pipeline, 1973
17	Queen Mary I of England died, 1558
18	William Tell shot apple off son's head, 1307
19	*Necessity sharpens industry.*
20	Yo-yo patented, 1866 • Photos required for U.S. passports, 1914
21	Harry Truman first U.S. president to travel underwater in sub, 1946
22	National Hockey League established, 1917
23	Author Roald Dahl died, 1990
24	Suspected JFK assassin Lee Harvey Oswald murdered, 1963
25	First sword-swallower performance in U.S., 1817
26	*Peanuts* cartoonist Charles Schulz born, 1925
27	Penn. Station in N.Y.C. opened, 1910
28	*Wonder is the seed of science.*
29	*Pong,* a coin-operated video game, debuted, 1972
30	Meteorite hit woman in her Ala. home, 1954

December

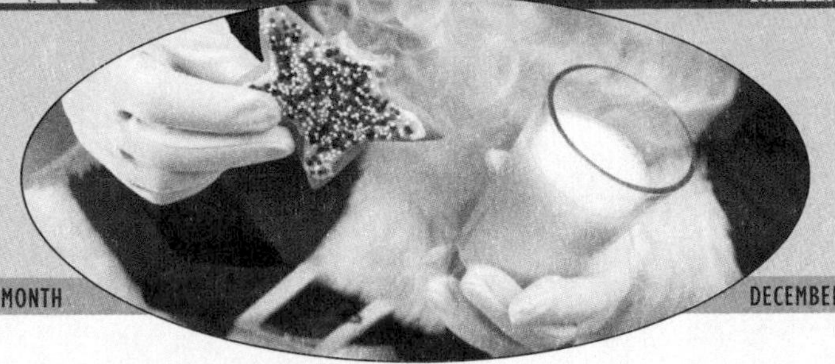

THE TWELFTH MONTH — DECEMBER HATH 31 DAYS

1	Scrabble trademark registered, 1948
2	"In God We Trust" promoter C. Bennett born, 1910
3	45.7 inches of snow fell on Denver, Colo., 1913
4	First TV appearance of French mime Marcel Marceau, 1955
5	U.S. president Martin Van Buren born, 1782
6	**St. Nicholas** • *No sweet without sweat.*
7	**National Pearl Harbor Remembrance Day**
8	"In Flanders Fields" poem published, 1915
9	Canada's first coin club formed, 1862
10	Miss. became 20th state, 1817
11	Arctic weather stopped London's Big Ben clock, 1981
12	Keiko the killer whale, star of *Free Willy,* died, 2003
13	**St. Lucia** • *One today is worth two tomorrows.*
14	*National Velvet* premiered, 1944
15	Philadelphia streets first cleaned by machine, 1854
16	Football player William "Refrigerator" Perry born, 1962
17	*The wise understand half a word.*
18	Singer Christina Aguilera born, 1980
19	Mark Twain received a patent for suspenders, 1871
20	Louisiana Purchase finalized, 1803
21	Crossword puzzle debuted in N.Y.C. newspaper, 1913
22	**Beware the Pogonip.** • Earthquake hit the Calif. coast, 2003
23	George Washington resigned army commission, 1783
24	Television host Ryan Seacrest born, 1974
25	**Christmas Day** • Actor Charlie Chaplin died, 1977
26	**Boxing Day (Canada)** • **First day of Kwanzaa**
27	*No man is a hero to his valet.*
28	Chewing gum was invented by a dentist, Mt. Vernon, Ohio, 1869
29	Gaslights first used at the White House, 1848
30	–48°F in Mazama and Winthrop, Wash., 1968
31	*With bounteous cheer, conclude the year.*

Almanac

Facts, folklore, and traditions t

January 1

New Year's Day. This month is named for the Roman god Janus, who has two faces. One face looks to the future and the other to the past, making a fitting symbol for this day.

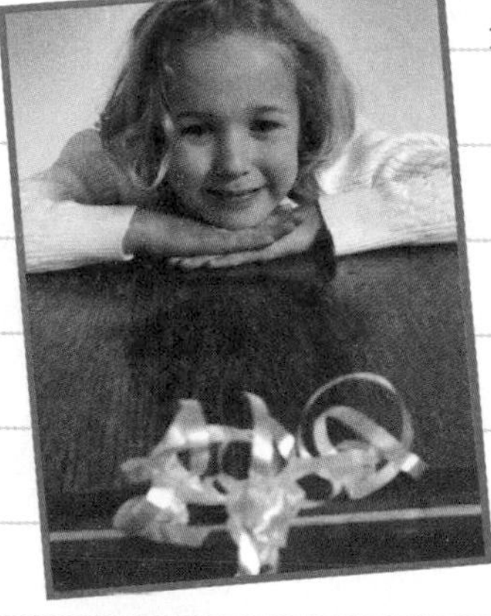

The first Monday: Handsel Monday. In Scotland in the 14th to 19th centuries, children and servants received a small gift, or handsel, on this day.

February 2

Groundhog Day. Traditionally, this was the day to prepare for spring planting. If it were sunny and a certain animal saw its shadow, people believed that winter weather would continue. In France and England, that animal was a bear. In Germany, it was a badger. In the 1800s, German immigrants to Pennsylvania found no badgers but lots of groundhogs, or woodchucks, so they adapted that species to the lore.

March 15

The ides of March. In the ancient Roman calendar, "the ides" marked the middle of some months. Ever since the assassination of Julius Caesar on this day in 44 B.C., the ides of March have been considered unlucky.

Oddities

CELEBRATE throughout the year.

April 1

All Fools' Day. Centuries ago in France, new-year celebrations started on March 25 (the first day of the new year, according to old calendars) and lasted until April 1. Starting in 1582, when New Year's Day was moved to January 1, it's said that people who didn't observe the change were made the butts of jokes on April 1.

The last Friday: National Arbor Day. When J. Sterling Morton moved to the Nebraska Territory in 1854, he noticed the lack of trees there. He planted some, both to beautify the area and preserve the soil. Other people did too, and Arbor Day was first celebrated in 1872. Plant a tree!

May 11 12 13

Three Chilly Saints. These days are often the coldest of the month. Because they are the feast days of the Christian saints Mamertus, Pancras, and Gervais, the days themselves have come to be known as the Three Chilly Saints.

June 14

Flag Day. The U.S. Continental Congress adopted the first official American flag on this day in 1777. Flag Day was first celebrated in 1877. In 1916, President Woodrow Wilson issued a proclamation that officially established this day as Flag Day.

July **1** **Canada Day.** Canada Day, so named by Parliament in 1982, commemorates the creation of the Dominion of Canada on this day in 1867.

3 **Dog Days begin.** Ancient Egyptians thought that the bright Dog Star, Sirius, in the constellation Canis Major, caused heat and droughts, sickness, and discomfort beginning today and lasting for 40 days (until August 11).

August **17** **Cat Nights commence.** Have you heard the saying "a cat has nine lives"? It is from an Irish legend about witches who turned themselves into cats and back into people eight times. On the ninth time, this day, they couldn't turn back.

September **23**

Harvest Home. Around September 23 in Europe, people celebrated the harvest with festivals and feasts on this day. Today, the Pennsylvania Dutch continue the tradition.

October 9

Leif Eriksson Day. The Viking voyager landed his boat on Newfoundland in the year 1000. He did not officially discover America, but the U.S. Congress honors him with this day.

November **The first Saturday:**

Sadie Hawkins Day. Cartoonist Al Capp invented this holiday for his comic strip "Li'l Abner." Today, it is an occasion for girls to ask boys to school dances and other events.

December 26

Boxing Day. In England, it was customary to give gift "boxes" to mailmen and servants on this day. Today, in Great Britain, Canada, and Australia, it is a day of rest.

The REASON fo

People puzzled over this fo

In one year, Earth revolves completely around the Sun while rotating on an invisible axis, like a tilted, spinning top. At one end of the axis is the North Pole; at the other, the South Pole. The axis is tilted at a 23.5-degree angle away from the Sun during winter in the Northern Hemisphere; it's the opposite during summer. Seasons are determined by the direction of Earth's tilt in relation to the Sun and the angle of the Sun's light as it strikes Earth.

The equator is an imaginary line dividing Earth into the Northern and Southern Hemispheres. On two days each year, on or around March 21 and September 23, the Sun is directly above the equator. In the Northern Hemisphere, spring starts on the March date, which is called the **vernal equinox;** fall begins on the September date, which is called the **autumnal equinox.**

Summer in the Northern Hemisphere begins on or around June 21, the **summer solstice,** when the Sun is directly above an imaginary line 23.5 degrees north of the

SEASONS

enturies. Not anymore!

summer

equator called the Tropic of Cancer. Winter begins on or around December 21, the **winter solstice,** when the Sun is above the Tropic of Capricorn, 23.5 degrees south of the equator.

The seasons are the opposite in the Southern Hemisphere.

The LONG and SHORT of It

- The summer solstice is one of the longest days of the year in the Northern Hemisphere—and the day when there is no sunlight at the South Pole.
- The winter solstice is one of the shortest days of the year in the Northern Hemisphere—and the day when there is no sunlight at the North Pole.
- Daytime and nighttime on the equinoxes are not equal; this is a myth. However, within a few days of each equinox, there is a day with nearly equal daytime and nighttime. (This depends on the latitude.)

You can find the exact time of day that the solstices and equinoxes occur at **Almanac4kids.com/sky.**

winter

CONTINUED

PARTY TIME

For centuries, people have watched the sky for the changes of season and then celebrated with colorful rituals.

SPRING

In India, many people celebrate the festival of Navroze, or "New Day," on the spring equinox. It is a day to clean and paint houses, wear new clothes, and hang jasmine flowers and roses on doors and windows.

SUMMER

In ancient times, women and girls in Sweden would bathe in a river in the belief that this would bring plenty of rain for the crops, while village people would dance around a decorated tree. Now, in late June, Swedes dance around a pole covered with greenery and flowers.

AUTUMN

The Chinese mark the end of summer with the Mid-Autumn Moon Festival, which occurs when the Moon is at its brightest. After dark, people stroll with brightly lit lanterns, admire the full Moon, and eat moon cakes, which are pastries with a whole egg yolk in the center symbolizing the Moon.

WINTER

Ancient Romans welcomed winter with the festival of Saturnalia, honoring Saturn, the god of agriculture. People decorated their houses with evergreen branches and lit lamps all night to ward off the darkness. Around the time of the solstice, in ancient Scandinavia, people hung mistletoe and evergreens in doorways for good luck and then gathered around bonfires to listen to singing poets. They believed that the fires would help the Sun shine more brightly.

It's About TIME

Every year on the summer solstice, thousands of people travel to Stonehenge, England, a place with huge stones that were arranged in a circle around 3000 B.C. The huge monument celebrates the relation between the Sun and the seasons.

CONTINUED

Here are some other ANCIENT SEASONAL MARKERS:

- At what is now **CHICHÉN ITZÁ** ("CHEE-chen EET-sa"), **MEXICO,** Mayans built a huge pyramid around the year 1000. The play of the Sun's light on it signals the beginning of the seasons. On the spring equinox, for example, the light pattern looks like a snake. Mayans called this day "the return of the Sun serpent."

- In today's **CHACO CANYON, NEW MEXICO,** Anasazi Indians, who were expert sky watchers, carved spiral designs into rock to track the seasons and record the passage of time. This petroglyph is called the Sun Dagger because of the way the Sun's wedge-shape beams strike it in midday during the solstices.

The Sun Dagger at the summer solstice . . .

. . . and at the winter solstice.

- Around 3200 B.C., ancient people in **IRELAND** built a huge mound of dirt and surrounded it with stones. Today, the knoll is called **NEWGRANGE.** For five days over the winter solstice period, a beam of sunlight illuminates a small room inside the mound for 17 minutes at dawn. The room holds only 20 people at a time. Every year, thousands enter a lottery in hope of being one of the 100 people allowed to enter.

Travel in Time ➧ Take a moment to see these ancient sites and tell other kids how you mark the seasons at **Almanac4kids.com/tellus.**

A MONTH OF MOONS

NEW

FIRST QUARTER

WAXING

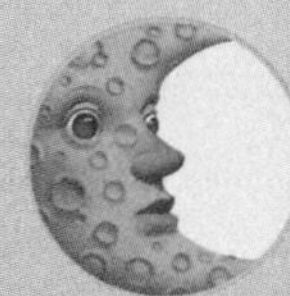

FULL

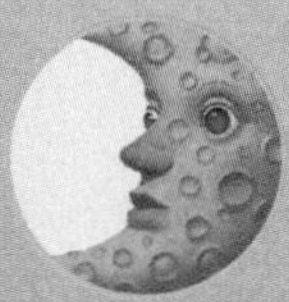

LAST QUARTER

WANING

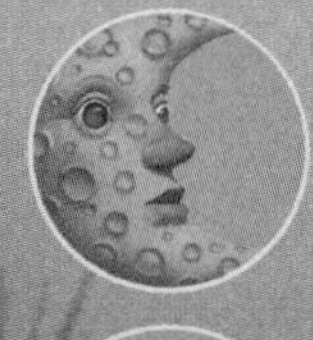

NEW

- The phases of the Moon reflect how it is illuminated when the Sun, Earth, and Moon are in different positions.
- When the Moon is between Earth and the Sun, the Sun's light shines on the side of the Moon that faces away from Earth. The Moon is almost invisible and is in its new phase. This begins the *waxing* period.
- When Earth is between the Sun and the Moon, the Sun's light shines directly on the side of the Moon that faces Earth. The Moon is in its full phase. This begins the *waning* period.
- The average length of a lunar month (from one new Moon to the next new Moon) is 29 days, 12 hours, and 44 minutes.

ONCE UPON A MOON . . .

For centuries, people have looked at the full Moon and tried to find an image in it.

- Americans see a man in the Moon.
- Polynesians see a woman with a child in the Moon.
- Japanese see a rabbit in the Moon.
- Scandinavians see a boy and girl holding a water bucket in the Moon.
- Other cultures see a man with a bundle of sticks on his back, or a toad, or a giant.

Go to Almanac4kids.com/tellus and describe what you see.

Maria Mitchell
(1818–89)

CLAIM TO FAME:

She was the first American woman to discover a comet.

What in the world was 29-year-old Maria Mitchell doing on the roof of the Pacific Bank on the island of Nantucket, Massachusetts, on the night of October 1, 1847?

Maria had grown up on Nantucket. Her father loved astronomy, and she loved his many rooftop lessons. When she finished her formal education, she became a librarian on the island and studied astronomy in her spare time, which is the reason that she was on the roof. Maria had a telescope and she was on a mission. The king of Denmark had promised to give a gold medal to anyone who discovered a new comet that was not visible to the naked eye, and Maria wanted to find one.

That night she did. She got her medal, becoming the only woman and the first American to get one, and the comet—Comet Mitchell 1847VI—was named for her.

Maria later became a professor of astronomy at Vassar College, a school for women, where she taught for 25 years. She was the first woman elected to the American Academy of Arts and Sciences, and the first woman member of the American Association for the Advancement of Science.

SEE FOR YOURSELF

For Maria, seeing was everything. Her favorite question for students was, "Did you learn that from a book or did you observe it yourself?"

Henrietta Swan Leavitt

(1868–1921)

CLAIM TO FAME:

Her observations helped scientists measure the distance of stars beyond the Milky Way.

Henrietta Swan Leavitt didn't plan to be an astronomer. She liked music and studied it at Oberlin College in Ohio. Later, she returned to Massachusetts (her home state) to attend Radcliffe College, where she took an astronomy class. After graduating in 1892, she became a volunteer at the Harvard College Observatory. Henrietta's title was "human computer"; her job was to count the stars and record data about every star in the sky, including color, brightness, and position. She and the other "computers," mostly women, stared for hours at photographic negatives of stars on glass plates and took detailed notes—all for 25 cents per hour.

Henrietta loved her work. She developed a scale called the "Harvard Standard," which was used to measure the brightness of stars, and became interested in "variable stars"—those whose brightness changes regularly, in cycles. During her lifetime, she spotted 2,400 variables—about 10 percent of those known today.

Henrietta realized that the brightness cycles of variable stars were related to distance. Her discovery (known as the Period-Luminosity Law) meant that these stars could be used as a sort of cosmic yardstick. With this, she had found a way to measure beyond the Milky Way, at a time when some scientists thought that there was nothing there.

NOW YOU SEE HER . . .

For years, some people said that Henrietta's ghost haunted the Harvard Observatory, lighting the lamp on her desk late at night and stalking the stacks of photographic plates that she had spent her life studying.

After her death, other astronomers, such as Edwin Hubble, used Henrietta's law to prove that stars and galaxies do lie beyond the Milky Way.

(continued)

Venetia Burney Phair

(b. 1919)

CLAIM TO FAME:

At age 11, she gave the planet Pluto its name.

SEE HERE!

Venetia was not the first in her family to name a heavenly body. Her great uncle, Henry Madan, had suggested the names Phobos and Deimos, both from Greek mythology, for Mars's moons.

As a girl in England, Venetia Burney loved learning about Greek and Roman mythology. Little did she know that it would make her famous.

One morning in March 1930, Venetia came down to breakfast, where her grandfather, a retired university librarian, was reading the newspaper. He told her that on February 18, 1930, Clyde Tombaugh, an amateur astronomer working at the Lowell Observatory, in Flagstaff, Arizona, had discovered a new planet. Astronomers were calling it Planet X, but it needed a name.

Venetia thought for a moment and then said, "Why not call it Pluto?"

Pluto was the Greek god of the underworld. Venetia's grandfather liked the name. He had a friend who was an astronomy professor at the University of Oxford, so he told him about Venetia's idea. The professor then sent a telegram with Venetia's suggestion to the Lowell Observatory.

Many names had been suggested, but the astronomers liked Pluto. One reason was that the first two letters of the word were the initials of Percival Lowell, the Observatory's founder. (Percival had launched the search for the ninth planet but had died in 1916.)

More than a month passed. Venetia had almost forgotten about the planet. Then, in May 1930, her grandfather gave her the news that the planet had officially been named Pluto. He also gave her a reward of five pounds (British money).

Venetia later became a teacher. She doesn't talk much about her claim to fame. "It doesn't arise in conversation, and you don't just go around telling people that you named Pluto," she says.

Perplexing PLUTO

In 2006, astronomers reclassified Pluto as a "dwarf planet," but it is still considered to be one of the largest bodies in the Kuiper Belt, a band of icy objects at the edge of our solar system. We may know more in 2015, when a NASA probe named *New Horizons* (*right;* launched on January 19, 2006) is scheduled to reach Pluto.

In this NASA artist's depiction, Pluto (above left) *is viewed from one of its two possible, or "candidate," moons. At right is its only confirmed moon, Charon.*

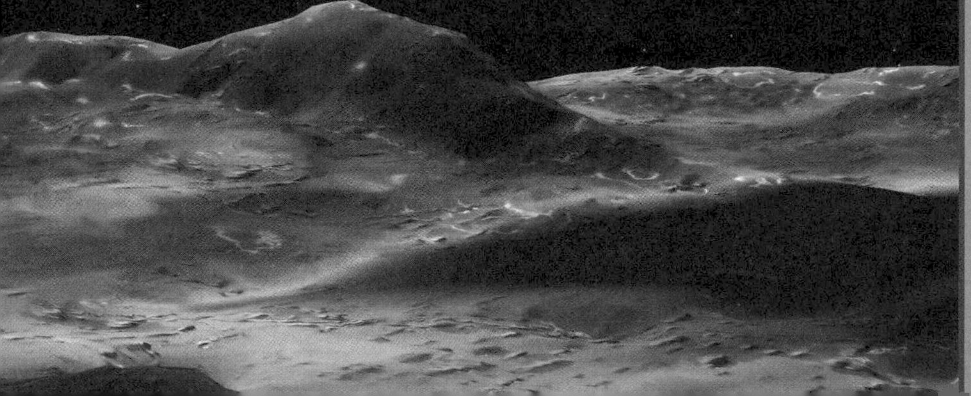

SATURN

The REAL Lord of the Rings

SATURN, the sixth planet from the Sun, is named for the Roman god of agriculture. In Greek mythology, Saturn became the ruler of the universe when he led a successful rebellion against his father, Uranus. Memorize these fast facts and you'll be a Saturn superstar.

GOTCHA! Galileo discovered Saturn in 1610.

BIG DEAL. Saturn is the second-largest planet in the solar system. (Jupiter is the largest.) More than nine Earths would fit across Saturn.

HOT ON THE INSIDE. Saturn's core temperature is about 21,150°F.

COLD ON THE OUTSIDE. The average temperature on Saturn is −280°F (that's w-a-a-a-y below zero).

HOLD ON TO YOUR HAT! Winds on Saturn blow at up to 1,100 miles per hour.

MOONSTRUCK. Saturn has 56 moons (and counting!). Titan is Saturn's largest moon and the second-largest one in the solar system.

FAR, FAR AWAY. Saturn is 885 million miles from the Sun, on average.

THINK UNSINKABLE. Saturn is the least dense of all the planets. If you could put Saturn into a huge swimming pool, it would float.

A LONG PASS. One year on Saturn equals about 29.5 years on Earth.

THE MAIN ATTRACTION. Saturn's magnetic field is 1,000 times stronger than the magnetic field on Earth.

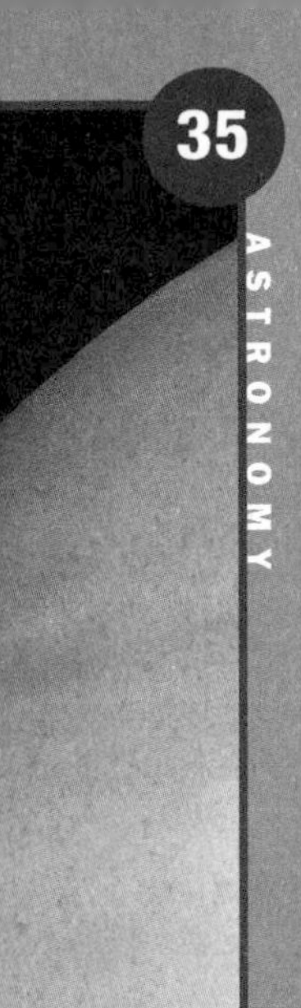

IT'S A GAS—MOSTLY. Saturn has a small, dense center surrounded by a layer of liquid and a very deep atmosphere. It is composed mostly of hydrogen and helium, with traces of water, ammonia, and methane.

A QUICK TURN. One day (including night) on Saturn equals 10 hours 47 minutes in Earth time. Because of this quick rotation and its gaseous composition, the planet's poles are flat.

RINGMASTER. Saturn is surrounded by unattached rings composed of billions of pieces of ice, dust, and rock ranging in size from as tiny as a grain of salt to as big as a house. The outermost ring may measure up to as much as 180,000 miles across.

BLAST OFF! Saturn has been visited by several probes (including *Pioneer 11*, and *Voyagers 1* and *2*). In 2004, *Cassini*, depicted above and named for French-Italian astronomer Jean-Dominique Cassini, started on a four-year mission to explore the planet, its rings, and its moons.

CATCH THE RINGS

Saturn will be especially visible in 2031. Can't wait? Go now to **Almanac4kids.com/sky** for close-up photos of the planet.

10 BURNING FACTS About the SUN

The Sun, with all those planets revolving around it and dependent upon it, can still ripen a bunch of grapes as if it had nothing else in the universe to do.

–Galileo Galilei, Italian astronomer (1564–1642)

1 THE SUN IS VERY OLD. The Sun is one of 100 billion stars in our Milky Way galaxy. Scientists estimate that the Sun is **about 4.5 billion years old,** or approximately halfway through its life cycle. Eventually, it is expected to become larger as it turns into a red giant, then shrink to a white dwarf, and then finally become a black dwarf, producing no heat or light.

2 THE SUN IS NOT SOLID. The Sun is composed of plasma, a material made from electrically charged gas atoms. It is **about 75 percent hydrogen** (the same flammable gas once used to fill airships such as the *Hindenburg* and now used in rocket fuel) and **about 25 percent helium** (the safer gas we now use to fill airships—and party balloons!). The remaining traces are tiny amounts of metals.

CONTINUED

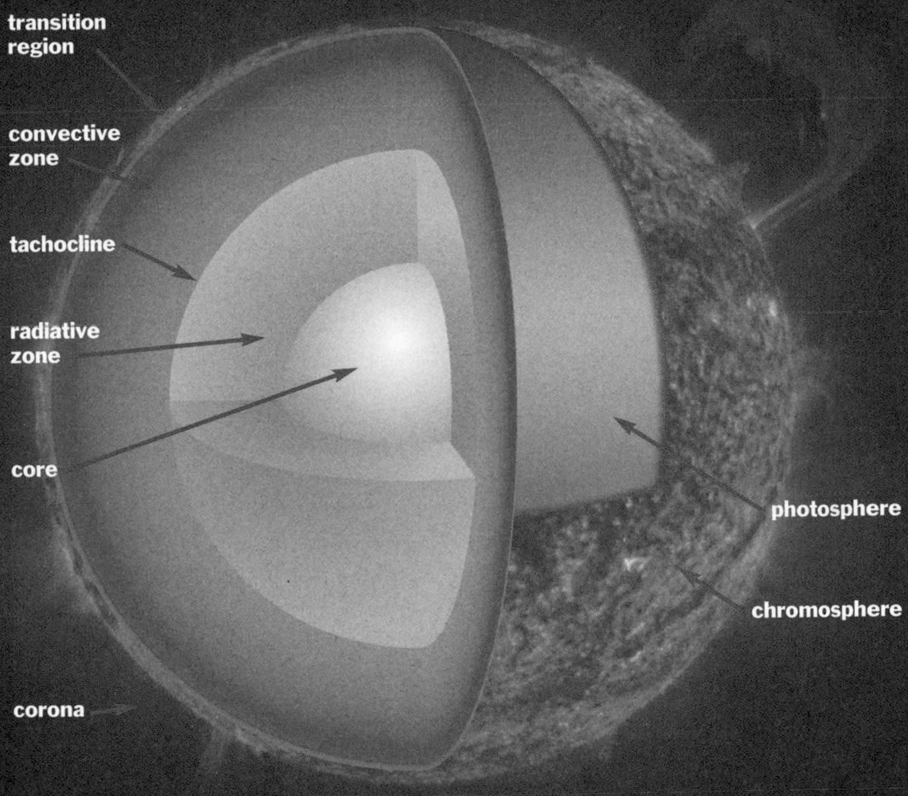

transition region
convective zone
tachocline
radiative zone
core
photosphere
chromosphere
corona

The SUN has 8 LAYERS:

CORE, the dense, hot center

RADIATIVE ZONE, where photon particles carry energy in all directions through a process called radiation

TACHOCLINE, a thin border between two differently rotating zones

CONVECTIVE ZONE, an area of boiling, bubbling plasma that transfers energy outward through a process called convection

PHOTOSPHERE, the visible surface, where sunspots appear

CHROMOSPHERE, a thin, reddish layer seen only during eclipses or with special solar-viewing equipment

TRANSITION REGION, between the hot corona and cooler chromosphere

CORONA, which extends far into space and is shaped by the Sun's magnetic field; it is visible only during eclipses or with special equipment

DID YOU KNOW?

The word "helium," for a gas first discovered on the Sun, came from Helios, the name for the Sun god in Greek mythology.

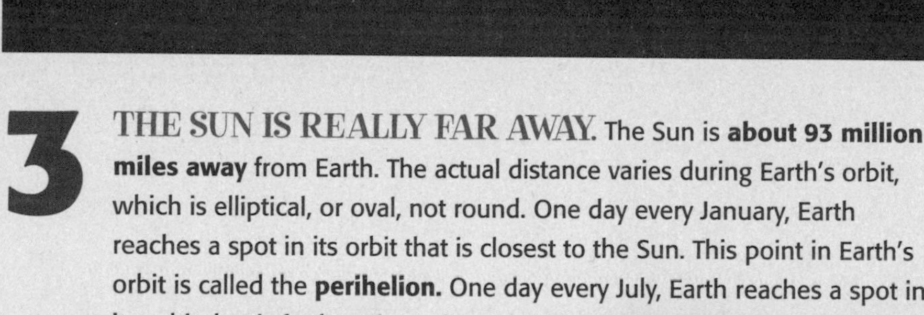

3 THE SUN IS REALLY FAR AWAY. The Sun is **about 93 million miles away** from Earth. The actual distance varies during Earth's orbit, which is elliptical, or oval, not round. One day every January, Earth reaches a spot in its orbit that is closest to the Sun. This point in Earth's orbit is called the **perihelion.** One day every July, Earth reaches a spot in its orbit that is farthest from the Sun. This point is called the **aphelion.**

4 THE SUN IS HUGE. The Sun is about 865,000 miles in diameter—that's **as wide as 109 Earths** placed side by side! About 1 million Earths would fit inside the Sun.

5 THE SUN MOVES VER-R-R-Y SLOWLY. The Sun is the center of our solar system, but it doesn't stay in one place. It orbits around the center of our Milky Way galaxy, which is about 28,000 light-years away. (A light-year is about 5.88 trillion miles.) It takes the Sun about **226 million years to go around the galaxy once!**

Approximate size of Earth

6 SECTIONS OF THE SUN SPIN AT DIFFERENT SPEEDS.

The Sun rotates on its axis in the same direction as Earth (counterclockwise, when looking down from the north pole). Because the Sun is gaseous, different sections rotate at different speeds. At the surface, **the area around the equator rotates once about every 25 days.** The Sun's north and south poles rotate more slowly. It can take those areas more than 30 days to complete one rotation.

7 THE SUN HAS A LOT OF PULL.

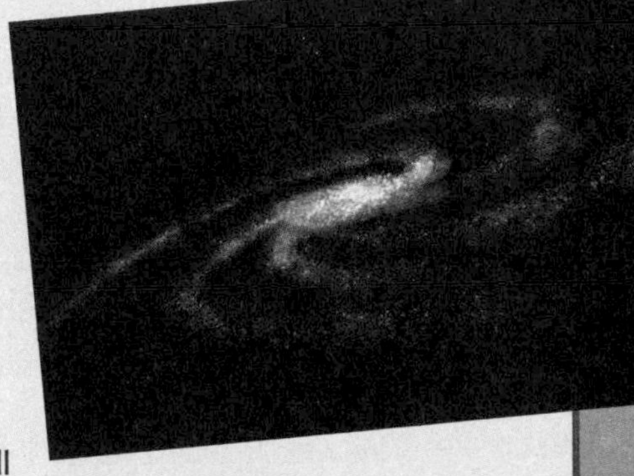

The Sun makes up more than 99 percent of the total mass of the solar system. Because it is so massive, the Sun exerts a lot of gravity, or pull, on the planets—enough to cause them to orbit around it. (If the planets were not themselves moving forward at a speed fast enough to balance the Sun's sideways pull, they would fall into the Sun.) **The Sun's gravity is about 27.9 times that of Earth,** and, in a small way, it helps to control the tides on Earth.

8 THE SUN IS A BALL OF ENERGY.

The Sun's core is under a lot of pressure. Because of this, hydrogen atoms are constantly colliding with each other at great speeds, fusing together to form helium, and releasing energy. Lots of these collisions occur, creating an enormous amount of energy. As a matter of fact, **in just one second, the Sun produces about 118 trillion times as much energy as the United States used in the year 2003!** Only about one-billionth of the total energy that the Sun produces reaches Earth, but it is enough to enable us to live here.

LOOK OUT!

Never look at the Sun without special protective eyewear. You can cause serious, permanent damage to your eyes.

CONTINUED

9 THE SUN IS HOT. The Sun's temperature varies over time and through its eight layers. **The hottest part of the Sun is the core, at 28,080,000°F, on average.** Moving outward, the next four layers become cooler. At the chromosphere, the temperature begins to rise again. The corona measures 1,800,000°F or more.

10 THE SUN HAS SPOTS. When the Sun's magnetic field pokes through the surface, it prevents the heat rising inside from coming through. As a result, the Sun's surface at these areas is cooler and darker than its surroundings, although still very bright. These dark areas are called sunspots. Sometimes, when the magnetic field suddenly breaks around a sunspot, plasma explodes into space. These **explosions, called solar flares and coronal mass ejections,** can cause magnetic storms that can temporarily knock out Earth's satellites, electricity, and communications, and pose a hazard to astronauts. Astronomers study sunspots to determine when these magnetic storms will occur. Scientists also examine how sunspots may affect Earth's climate. They look at . . .

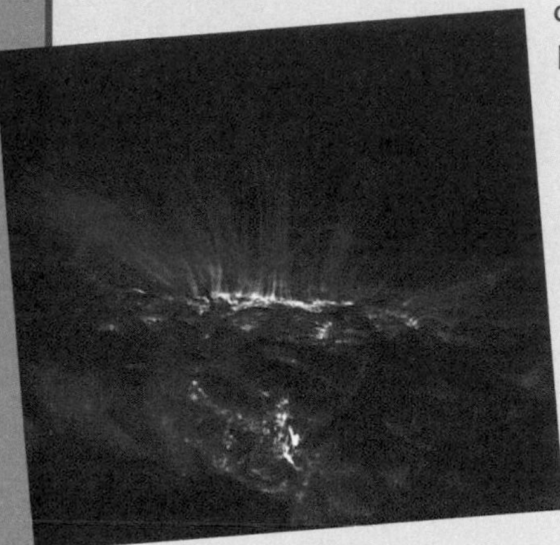

SUNSPOT SIZE:	Some sunspots are as big as Earth, while others are more than ten times that!
NUMBER:	The count varies; sunspots often appear in groups.
LIFE SPAN:	Each sunspot can last from a few hours to a few months.
CYCLE:	This is the periodic change in the frequency of sunspots, which usually occurs over about 11 years.

DID YOU KNOW?

***The Old Farmer's Almanac* uses sunspot activity to help in making its weather predictions.**

I wish I may, I wish I might

FIND MY OWN METEORITE!

Every day, dozens of small meteorites fall to Earth. Those that are seen coming down are called "falls." Those that are recovered on the ground are called "finds." If meteorites have landed in your backyard, you might be able to find them. Tape a strong magnet to the end of a broom handle. A meteorite contains a lot of iron, so it will stick to your magnet. Some ordinary rocks that contain a lot of iron will stick, too. You can tell a meteorite by its fusion crust, a thin, glassy coating that formed when the meteorite superheated during its fall through Earth's atmosphere.

OR VS. ITE **A METEOR is an object that has traveled through space and entered Earth's atmosphere. A METEORITE is a meteor that has reached Earth's surface without vaporizing.**

- In 1794, hundreds of people in Siena, Italy, observed a shower of stones fall from the sky. These were determined to be unlike any other rocks on Earth.
- Since 1978, teams of scientists have collected over 15,000 meteorite specimens from Antarctica. They are easier to find on that continent's snow-white surface.
- The largest meteorite ever found in the United States weighed 15 tons and was found in 1902 in Willamette, Oregon.
- One of Canada's most notable meteorites was found near Tagish Lake in northern British Columbia by Jim Brook on January 25, 2000. He almost mistook it for wolf poop.

STAR

URSA MINOR

BIG DIPPER

POLARIS

PEGASUS

pointer stars

URSA MAJOR

ORION

CANIS MAJOR

Note: Scale and orientation of constellations not exact

ART (AND A LITTLE SCIENCE)

DELPHINUS

Thousands of years ago, before TV, people spent hours looking at the night sky. They found that by connecting the stars as if they were dots, patterns emerged that resembled animals and people and things. Ancient civilizations attached myths and legends to the patterns. Eventually, 88 star patterns were identified. The patterns helped people tell the time of year and find their way on land and sea.

Today we call these star patterns constellations.

Constellations appear in different parts of the sky depending on the time of the day and year. (The stars don't move. Earth moves, rotating on its axis once every 24 hours and revolving around the Sun once every year.) Certain stars can help you find other stars and constellations. When you find a constellation, remember that it might not look exactly like the object it is named for. You have to use your imagination. Try it!

GETTING A HANDLE ON THE BIG DIPPER

This is not a constellation, but an asterism (a familiar group of stars located within a constellation). The Big Dipper has seven major stars: four in the "bowl" and three in the "handle." The two stars on the outside of the bowl are called the "pointer" stars. They point to Polaris, a bright star that is also called the North Star because with it you can figure out which way is north.

TO FIND NORTH: Find the Big Dipper. Find the pointer stars. Find Polaris. Look straight up. Turn your body toward Polaris. Now, you're facing north. (Runaway slaves used Polaris to find their way to Canada during the Civil War.)

USE YOUR FISTS

Astronomers use a closed fist at arm's length to measure the distance between stars. For example, it's three fists from the Big Dipper to Polaris, the North Star. (If your hands are small, it might be more.)

URSA MAJOR, the Great Bear

If you find the Big Dipper, you have found the Great Bear: The Dipper's handle is the Bear's tail. Can you find the rest of the Bear? (Use your imagination!) Legends about the Great Bear abound. Ancient Greeks and Romans believed that a mythological king grabbed its tail, swung it around, and flung it into the sky to whirl around the North Pole forever. Some Native Americans believed that the three tail stars were hunters chasing the Bear.

URSA MINOR, the Little Bear

Polaris will help you find the Little Dipper, also known as Ursa Minor, or the Little Bear. Polaris is the star on the end of the Little Dipper's handle.

ORION, the Hunter

This is easiest to find in winter. Look for three bright stars in a line—these are Orion's belt. The two stars north of this are his shoulders. One of these is Betelgeuse ("BEETLE-juice"), which is a red giant star. The two brighter stars to the south are in his legs.

Ancient people used Orion to predict the seasons: If it appeared at midnight, the grapes were ready to harvest. If it appeared in the morning, summer was beginning. If it appeared in the evening, winter had arrived.

CANIS MAJOR, the Great Dog

This is named for the larger of Orion's two hunting dogs (the other, Canis Minor, has only two stars). To find Canis Major,

STAR-T THINKING!

On a clear night, when there is no moonlight, spend some time looking at the sky. Connect some stars to make an original constellation. Draw it and make up a story about it. Share your story with other kids at **Almanac4kids.com/tellus.**

imagine a straight line through Orion's belt. Move your eyes left (south) until you come to a very bright star—that's Sirius, the nose of the dog. Look farther south to find a triangle of stars that marks the dog's hindquarters.

Ancient Egyptians called Sirius "the Nile Star" because it always appeared in the sky right before summer began and the waters of the River Nile began to flood. In medieval Europe, people thought that a combination of light from the Sun and Sirius caused the hot and humid "dog days" of summer.

DELPHINUS, the Dolphin

This is faint and looks like a kite. According to one legend, when dolphins convinced a sea goddess to marry Poseidon, the sea god, he named a constellation after them. Look for this in the summer.

PEGASUS, the Winged Horse

The secret to finding this is to know that its four stars make a square. The clearest view of it is in October, but it is visible from July through January. According to Greek myth, Pegasus carried thunder and lightning for the god Zeus.

STAR STATS

On a clear and moonless night away from bright lights, you can see about 2,500 stars.

Though all stars are hot, a star's color depends on its temperatures. "Hot" stars are bluish, "warm" ones are white, and "cool" ones are yellow, orange, or red.

Stars are different sizes. Dwarf stars are 1,000 times smaller than the Sun, while super giants may be 1,000 times bigger than the Sun.

You may not believe it, but there were no dandelions in North America before the early settlers arrived. They brought dandelion seeds, along with many other plant seeds, with them. The settler women used almost every part of the plant. They used the young green leaves in salads and stews and steeped them in hot water to make tea. They sliced and cooked its thick white roots to eat as a vegetable or dried, ground, and roasted them to make a beverage. With the flower heads, they made wine or a yellow dye for wool clothing.

Today, many people don't like dandelions because they can not rid their lawns of them. The plant's main root, or taproot, can be up to 3 feet long. If you dig up a dandelion but leave even a piece of the root, the plant will

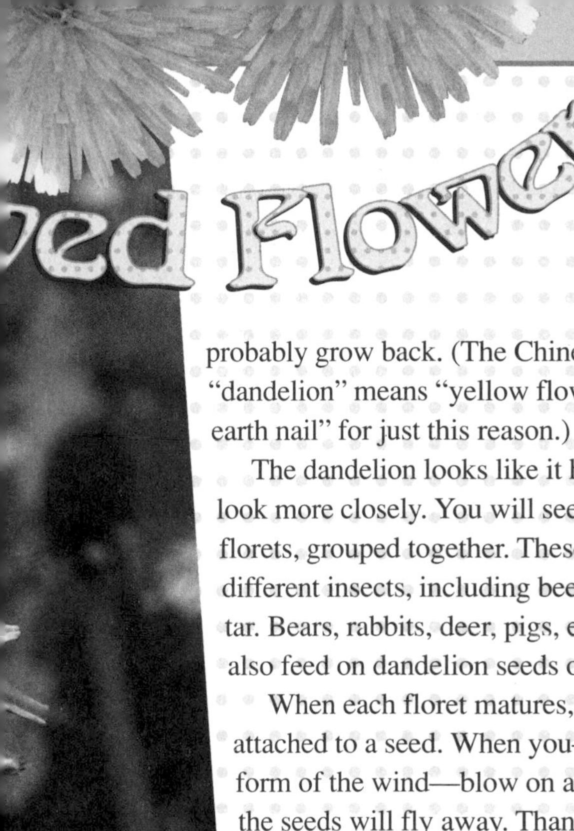

probably grow back. (The Chinese for "dandelion" means "yellow flower earth nail" for just this reason.)

The dandelion looks like it has one big yellow flower—but look more closely. You will see as many as 200 tiny flowers, or florets, grouped together. These flowers are food for at least 93 different insects, including bees that take the pollen and nectar. Bears, rabbits, deer, pigs, elk, mice, goats, and many birds also feed on dandelion seeds or leaves.

When each floret matures, it produces a tiny parachute attached to a seed. When you—or Mother Nature, in the form of the wind—blow on a parachute ball (the seed head), the seeds will fly away. Thanks to their parachutes, some seeds will land gently. Other seeds will be carried away on clothing and on animal fur and dropped or rubbed off far from the mother plant.

(continued)

Dan-de-licious!

* Dandelion greens contain vitamins A, B, and C, plus protein, calcium, phosphorus, iron, potassium, and sodium. You can buy young dandelion greens for salads in food markets. (Old dandelion leaves taste bitter.) Or, if your lawn is free of chemical fertilizers, pick some dandelion greens from your own yard.

* Avoid eating dandelion greens growing by the side of the road. They may have been exposed to chemical fertilizers or harmful auto emissions.

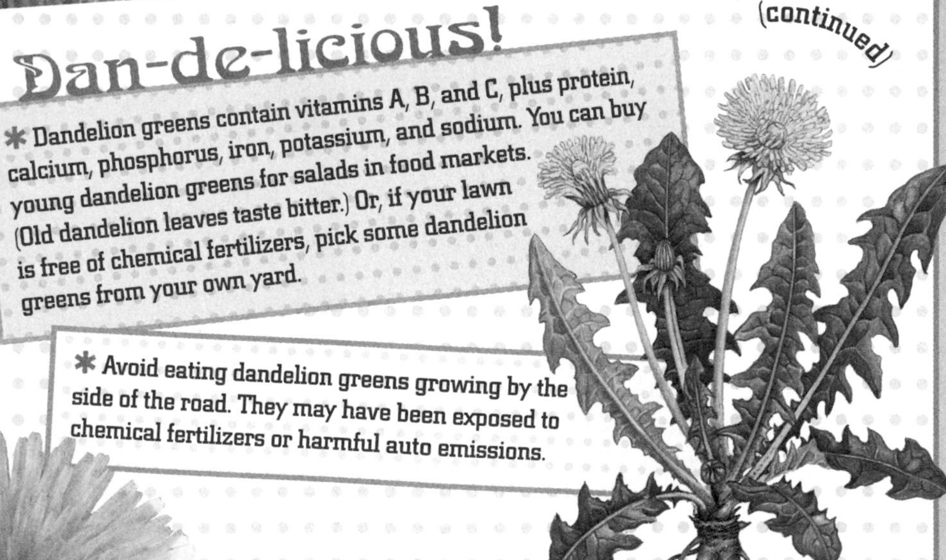

Just Say DANDY

The dandelion has many names. In France long ago, people thought that the plant's jagged leaves looked like lion's teeth, so they called the plant *dent de lion,* or "tooth of the lion." In North America, *dent de lion* became "dandelion."

People used to call the dandelion the face clock or shepherd's clock because it was believed to tell time.

Try it:

* Blow on a seed head three times. Count the seeds remaining. That's the correct hour.
* Count the number of puffs it takes to blow off all the seeds. That's the correct hour.

The dandelion has been called the fortune-teller because blowing on a seed head was believed to be a way to predict events. Try it:

* Make a wish, then blow. If all the seeds come off at once, your wish will come true.
* Think of someone you like, then blow. If all the seeds come off at once, that person likes you, too.
* The number of puffs it takes to remove all the seeds is the number of years it will be before you are married.

The dandelion's other nicknames come from its appearance:

BLOWBALL or **PUFFBALL**
for its shape and airy seeds

GOAT'S BEARD
what a seed head looks like when turned upside down

MONK'S HEAD
what a seedless head was thought to look like in medieval times

SWINE SNOUT
what a mature flower looks like when closed up

Other 'Chuters

These plants also have parachute-style seeds, although each is different:

- clematis
- hawkweed
- wild lettuce
- milkweed
- thistle

milkweed

thistle

A Gardener's Worst Fears

You may have heard the word *arachnophobia,* which means fear of *spiders.* A phobia is a fear of something. Here are some phobias related to weather and gardening.

OBJECT FEARED	NAME OF FEAR
Ants	Myrmecophobia
Bees	Apiphobia or Melissophobia
Birds	Ornithophobia
Compost (garbage and decaying material)	Seplophobia
Dirt	Rupophobia
Flowers	Anthophobia
Frogs	Ranidaphobia
Frost	Pagophobia
Garlic	Alliumphobia
Insects	Entomophobia or Insectophobia
Leaves	Phyllophobia
Moths	Mottephobia
Mushrooms	Mycophobia
Parasites	Parasitophobia
Plants	Batonophobia
Rain	Ombrophobia
Toads	Bufonophobia
Trees	Dendrophobia
Vegetables	Lachanophobia
Wasps	Spheksophobia
Worms	Scoleciphobia

A Prickly Subject

There are more than 2,000 species of cactus in the world, and they exist in a variety of shapes and sizes. Some are shaped like pincushions, some like starfish, and some like blades of grass. Others, like "beavertail" and "organ pipe," are named for their unusual shapes. Most cacti live in hot, dry places, but some grow in rain forests, on grasslands, or in high mountains—even near Antarctica.

Most cacti have prickly spines instead of leaves. The spines can be short or long, soft or sharp. Spines protect cacti from animals that want to eat or take water from them.

Cacti produce flowers. Most are large, colorful blooms to attract the insects that pollinate them. In the desert, most flowers open at night when it's cool and close during the day.

Cacti need water to survive. Some rain forest cacti have roots in the air to collect rain as it falls. Desert cacti absorb moisture through roots that can be 10 to 15 feet long and lie just below the soil. Some cacti can go without water for weeks—or longer. Prickly pear cacti can survive for nine to ten months without water. The saguaro cactus can survive on stored water for four to five years.

A cactus "breathes" through stomata, which are tiny openings (similar to our sweat glands) in the plant's waxy skin. Stomata remain closed during the day so that the plant doesn't lose too much moisture. They open after sunset, when temperatures cool down.

Cacti Facti

- One plant is a "cactus." Many plants are **"cacti"** or **"cactuses."**

- A cactus plant can produce a **million seeds,** but only one or two live long enough to produce a new cactus.

- In their natural environment, some cactus plants can **live for 50 to 200 years.**

- The **world's tallest cactus** is the giant saguaro *(Carnegiea gigantea),* which grows in the Sonoran Desert in Arizona, in southern California, and in Mexico. It can grow to be 50 feet tall and weigh up to eight tons.

- The **saguaro cactus blossom** is Arizona's state flower.

- The **world's tiniest cactus** is the almost half-inch-tall *Blossfeldia liliputana,* which can be found growing in cracks between rocks in Bolivia. During the dry season, the stems lose almost all of their water and shrink, becoming almost completely flat.

- The **cactus wren** builds its nest in the middle of the spines of the cholla ("CHOY-ya") cactus, found in deserts in the U.S. Southwest. In the Sonoran Desert, gila ("HEE-la") woodpeckers and gilded flickers carve nesting holes in saguaro cacti instead of trees.

- **Desert pack rats** go inside cacti to hide from predators. The tiny rats make tunnels in the cacti and burrow inside them, nesting among bits of string, twigs, feathers—almost anything that they can "pack" in.

STUCK ON THIS?
Go to Almanac4kids.com/outdoors for links to National Parks with lots of cacti.

BEANS

Bountiful Beans!

People have been planting and eating beans forever. They are easy to grow and they are good for you. Try it and see! The best time to plant beans is in spring. Even if you don't harvest any edible beans, you'll have a "vine" time trying!

You will need:

- 10 to 15 bean seeds
- Styrofoam or double-thick (hot beverage) paper cups (8 ounces), or peat pots if you plan to transplant the seedlings to a garden
- a pen
- scrap paper and tape (optional)
- potting soil
- drinking straws

Decide what types of beans you would like to grow and go to a gardening store to buy the seeds. Bush beans grow like bushes, up to 2 feet tall. Pole beans need something to climb and can grow 8 feet tall or even taller. Pick several bean types that you like and plan to plant two or three beans of each.

1. Put the seeds into a small bowl. Add enough water to cover. Soak them overnight.

2. Write the name of each type of bean on each cup. Or write the names on small pieces of paper and attach a piece of paper to each cup.

3 Fill each cup about two-thirds full of soil.

4 Place two or three of the same type of bean seeds on the soil in each cup.

5 Cover the seeds with about a half-inch of soil.

6 Using a spoon, add water gently to each cup. Stop when the top inch of the soil is damp. Too much water will drown the beans.

7 Put the cups in a sunny window.

In about a week, green stems with leaves will appear. Add enough water to keep the soil slightly damp. The plants will grow toward the Sun. Turn the cups a little each day so that the vines will grow straight up.

CONTINUED

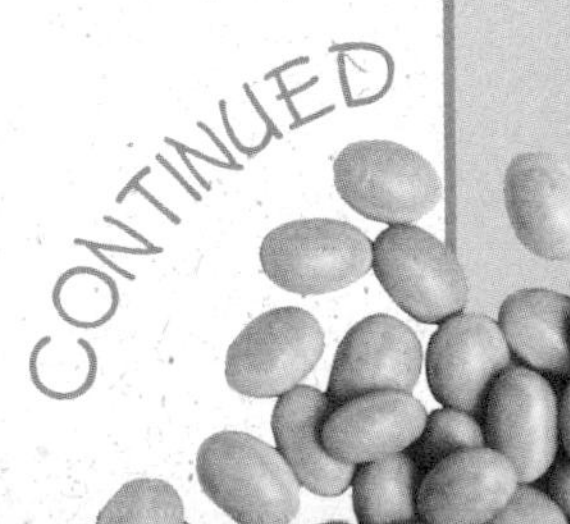

When you plant pole bean seeds or when the pole bean plants are about 2 inches tall, push a drinking straw into the soil—but carefully, so that you do not smash the roots. As the bean vines grow, they will need taller supports, such as a lightweight bamboo pole, a cut and stretched out coat hanger, or a string attached to the ceiling. (If you want to do the string thing, be sure to ask your parents.)

With care, sun, and enough moisture, your bean plant may live up to a year if kept indoors. You can also transplant it to the garden when all danger of frost has passed and the soil has warmed. If you've used peat pots, bury the entire container in the soil without disturbing the bean roots. If you've used cups, gently remove the soil and roots from each container and transplant them into an appropriate hole.

As your bean plants get taller, look for flowers and bean pods. It takes about 8 weeks for pods to appear.

SPILL YOUR BEANS

Write a short story about your bean plants and share it with other kids at Almanac4kids.com/tellus.

Every BEAN Counts

Beans were used in elections centuries ago:

Ancient Romans used black beans to cast "no" votes and white beans to cast "yes" votes.

Members of secret societies in ancient Greece voted for or against admitting new members by dropping differently colored beans into jars or helmets. If someone accidentally tipped over the container and revealed the secret vote, this was called "spilling the beans."

Hill o' Beans

The Latin family name for beans is *Leguminosae*.

There are over 13,000 known bean varieties in the world. Many beans have names that reveal their history or hint at what they look like. Here are a few that you can throw around with your friends:

ANASAZI BEANS were grown by the Anasazi Native Americans as early as A.D. 130.

BUMBLEBEE BEANS, originally from Maine, are large white seeds with a black mark.

CAVE BEANS were found sealed in a clay pot in New Mexico and later scientifically dated to be 1,500 years old.

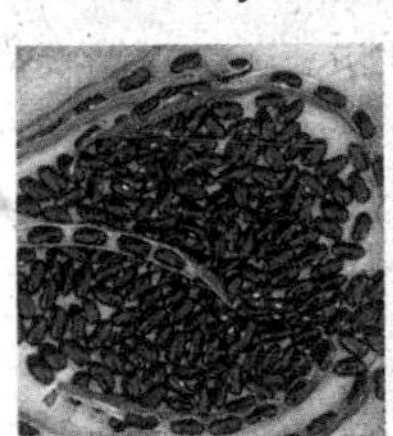

CHEROKEE TRAIL OF TEARS BEANS were carried by Cherokee Native Americans on the Trail of Tears march from Georgia to Oklahoma in 1838 and 1839. (For more about this event, turn to "The First Great Gold Rush," beginning on page 116.)

CIVIL WAR BEANS were brought to Kentucky by a Civil War veteran returning home in 1860.

LAFAYETTE BEANS were brought from France to Rhode Island by the Marquis de Lafayette around 1776, and named after him.

LAZY HOUSEWIFE BEANS do not require destringing. They were brought by German immigrants to Pennsylvania around 1810.

MARROW FAT BEANS were a staple of Civil War soldiers in the 1860s. Some say that they taste a little like bacon.

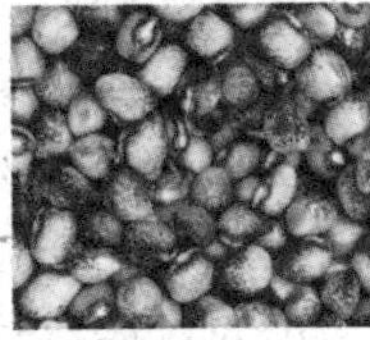

MAYFLOWER BEANS are believed to have been brought to America by the Pilgrims on the *Mayflower* in 1620.

MOSTOLLER'S WILD GOOSE BEANS were discovered, so the story goes, in the crop—a pouch in a bird's throat—of a goose by members of a Pennsylvania family named Mostoller around 1865.

PETALUMA GOLD RUSH BEANS were brought to the San Francisco area from Peru during the Gold Rush and sold in the mining camps.

VERACRUZANO BEANS were brought by Mexican soldiers to the United States during the Mexican War of 1846.

VERMONT CRANBERRY BEANS, a New England variety believed to date from 1797, are streaked and spotted with burgundy.

WREN'S EGG BEANS are the smallest of the cranberry-type beans, resembling tiny bird's eggs.

Who says that you can't have a garden in the winter?

Grow a Vege

YOU WILL NEED:

- 2 carrots (fat ones, if possible)
- 2 beets
- 1 small rutabaga
- 1 small turnip
- 1 or more radishes
- a glass pie dish or pan
- paring knife

Use vegetables that are fresh, not soft and squishy. Look for some that have a tiny bit of green at the stem end.

1 Cut off this much of the vegetables at the stem end: 2 inches of the carrot tops; 1½ inches of the beet tops; 1 inch each of the rutabaga, turnip, and radish tops. (Ask an adult to help you if necessary.)

2 Put the vegetable bottoms into the refrigerator. (Your family can eat those later.)

3 Fill the dish with 1 to 2 inches of cool water.

4 Put the vegetable tops into the dish on their flat ends. (Do not scrub the vegetable tops or wash them in hot water before.)

5 Put the dish near a sunny window.

able Forest

Make sure that there is always about 1 inch of water in the pan. (Change the water if it becomes cloudy.) In about a week, green leaves will begin to grow out of the vegetable tops. Little white threads might also emerge from the veggie tops. These are rootlets. Leave them alone.

The green leaves get nutrition from the vegetable tops. In about a month, when this food supply is used up, fewer leaves appear. The existing leaves will wilt and dry up. When that happens, throw out the tops and start another batch. You can try growing other vegetables too, such as celery and parsnip.

Harvest Handfuls

Match the vegetables with their leaf color and shape:

Veggies	Leaves
1. BEET	**a.** medium green and feathery
2. CARROT	**b.** bluish green, rounded with curves
3. RADISH	**c.** bright light green, hairy, egg-shape with curves
4. RUTABAGA	**d.** medium green with red veins, round and crinkly
5. TURNIP	**e.** dark green, round and crinkly

Turn the page to find the answers

Veggie Bites

Beets can be red, purple, white, or yellow. Some beets have red and white stripes. A Scottish beet has metallic-purple leaves.

Radishes can be white, gold, dark purple, rose, red, or black. A German white radish can grow as big as a turnip.

In America in the 1600s, women stuck long, feathery, wild carrot leaves in their hats for decoration.

Years ago, in Europe, children celebrated Halloween by carving faces into large turnips—not pumpkins.

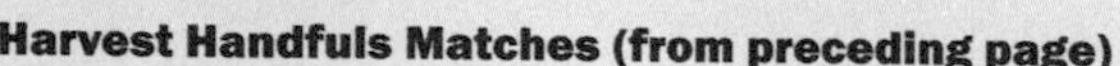

Harvest Handfuls Matches (from preceding page)

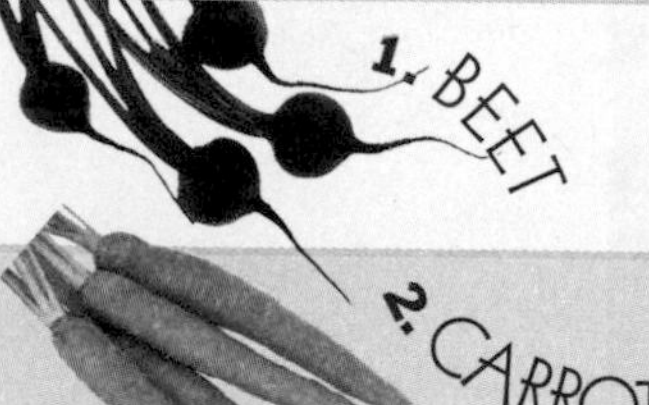

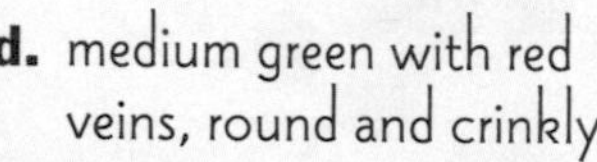

d. medium green with red veins, round and crinkly

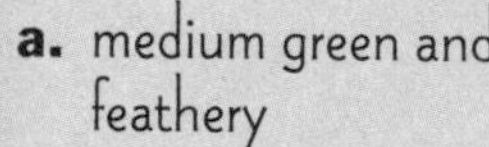

a. medium green and feathery

e. dark green, round and crinkly

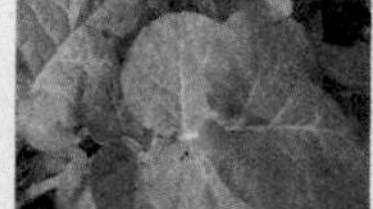

b. bluish green, rounded with curves

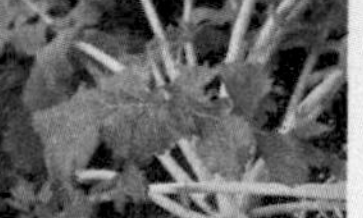

c. bright light green, hairy, egg-shape with curves

An Earful About corn

KERNELS OF KNOWLEDGE

One bushel of corn . . .

- **contains about 72,800 kernels and weighs 56 pounds.**
- **sweetens more than 400 cans of soda.**
- **makes enough oil for two pounds of margarine.**
- **makes enough starch for a ton of paper.**

Corn is grown on every continent except Antarctica.

Each ear of corn contains 600 to 800 kernels.

Popcorn was first introduced to English colonists by Native Americans on February 22, 1630.

Dr. John Kellogg served the world's first cornflakes to his patients in Battle Creek, Michigan, on March 7, 1897.

Q. What did the baby corn ask the mother corn?
A. Where is my pop corn?

Q. Why shouldn't you tell secrets on the farm?
A. Because the corn has ears, the potatoes have eyes, and the beanstalk.

LORE TO LIVE BY

Proverbs are often short lessons. What lessons would you learn from these?

- **Plant corn early or lose a bushel a day past the middle of May.**
- **Plow deep while sluggards sleep, and you will have corn to sell or keep.**
- **When the corn wears a heavy coat, so must you.**

Whoopee! It's Watermelon Time!

Watermelons date from about 5,000 years ago. They are believed to have first grown in the Kalahari Desert in southern Africa. Ancient Egyptians loved watermelons. They adorned buildings with drawings of them and often buried the pharaohs with watermelon seeds in the belief that the rulers would have nourishment in the afterlife. A watermelon is about 92 percent water; early explorers used the fruit as a water canteen. People living in dry climates still use watermelons as a source of water.

Square Fare

Be the first one on your "block" to grow a square watermelon!

1. In your garden, plant a seed or seedling for a small (5- to 15-pound) watermelon.

2. Get a rectangular cinder block.

3. When your melon is pea-size on the vine, place your cinder block so that the little melon hangs over one of the holes in the block.

4. Fertilize and water your watermelon plant as it grows.

5. When the watermelon is ripe and snugly fills the inside of the cinder block hole, break the cinder block with a sledge-hammer and remove the watermelon. (Get an adult to help you.)

6. Take a picture, then slice and serve!

Spitting for Fun

In 1989, the world record for spitting watermelon seeds was set by Lee Wheelis, who spit a seed 68 feet 9⅛ inches at the Luling (Texas) Watermelon Thump Festival. Watermelon seed-spitting contests are fun. Have one with your friends and share your distance record with other kids at **Almanac4kids.com/tellus.**

Take Your Pick

There are more than 1,200 varieties of watermelon in the world, and over 200 of these are grown in the United States and Mexico.

- **Watermelons can be round like a ball, oval like an egg, or oblong like a blimp.**
- **The skin can be yellow, light green, gray-green, dark green, or almost black; all one color, striped, marbled, or spotted. 'Moon and Stars' has a dark green skin with tiny, yellow "stars" and larger spots that look like moons.**
- **The pulp can be red, pink, yellow, orange, or white.**
- **The seeds can be black, white, brown, red, or speckled, and one watermelon can have as many as 1,000 seeds.**
- **Watermelons usually weigh between 5 and 40 pounds, depending on the type. Bill Carson of Arrington, Tennessee, grew a 262-pounder that held the world record from 1995–2005, when Lloyd Bright's 268.8-pounder grown in Hope, Arkansas, broke the record.**

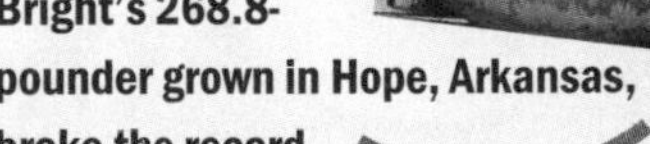

Freeze as you Please

Scrape the pulp from a watermelon and remove the seeds. Mash the pulp in a blender or food processor. Pour the mashed pulp into ice cube trays and freeze. Use the cubes to chill juice. Or, for melt-in-your-mouth melon pops, plunge wooden sticks into the mashed pulp before it freezes in the trays.

EAT DIRT? Yecchh!

At some point in time, people from every culture in the world (except maybe Eskimos) have accepted the custom of eating dirt.

The practice of eating dirt is called geophagy ("jee-OFF-uh-jee"); for some reason, it is done mostly by women. Geophagy dates from the ancient Greeks, who believed that dirt mixed with goat's blood was powerful medicine. Egg-shape balls of clay are still sold in some West African markets, and you might even see boxes of dirt for sale at back-road stands in the southern United States.

Not just any dirt will do. Loamy, clay soil from the hills is preferred to dirt from a riverbed. It is eaten raw or baked, with salt or vinegar added, for taste. Some experts believe that people who eat dirt crave minerals in their diet. Others say that it satisfies a desire for food that is crunchy and salty, such as when people crave potato chips.

Eating dirt may be a common custom, but this doesn't make it a good idea. Eating dirt can be dangerous; it may contain harmful chemicals.

To sample "soil" that is safe and delicious, make a Dirt Cake!

DIRT CAKE

Cake:

1 package (1 pound 2 ounces) Oreo cookies
1/4 cup (1/2 stick) margarine
8 ounces cream cheese, softened
1 cup confectioner's sugar
3 1/2 cups milk
2 packages (3.4 ounces each) instant vanilla pudding mix
12 ounces Cool Whip or similar dessert topping (but not whipped cream)

Presentation:

a clean, new, 8-inch, plastic flowerpot
wax paper
gummy worms, to mix in and for decoration
aluminum foil
plastic flowers and a clean, new, gardening tool

Crush the Oreo cookies by hand or in a food processor or blender. Set the crumbs aside. Put the margarine, cream cheese, and sugar into a large bowl. With a spoon or electric beater, mix these ingredients until they are blended and creamy. In a separate bowl, add the milk, pudding, and dessert topping. Mix these ingredients until they are blended. Add this mixture to the large bowl. Stir or beat everything together. Mix in gummy worms if you wish.

Line the bottom of the flowerpot with the dessert topping lid or wax paper. Add enough crushed cookies to make a 1-inch layer. Add a 1-inch layer of pudding mixture. Continue making layers, ending with crushed cookies. Decorate the pot with plastic flowers (wrap the stems in aluminum foil before planting), gummy worms, and a gardening tool. Refrigerate for at least 4 hours. When it's time to eat, remove the flowers, then serve with the tool. Put the pot back into the refrigerator after serving, if there is any "dirt" left over.

HEY, EWE!

Counting Sheep?

- A female sheep is a **EWE.**
- A male sheep is a **RAM.**
- A baby sheep is a **LAMB.**
- A one-year-old sheep is a **HOGGET.**
- A two-year-old sheep is a **TWO-TOOTH.**
- A group of sheep is a **FLOCK** or **MOB.**

When sheep collect and huddle,
Tomorrow will become a puddle.

Sheep have been raised on farms to provide meat, milk, and wool for more than 10,000 years. Today, there are about 800 different breeds of domesticated sheep and about 1 billion sheep on Earth—and you will almost never see one by itself. These gentle animals don't like to be alone. They have poor eyesight and are easily frightened. They flock together for companionship and protection.

Sheep have an excellent sense of hearing. A baby lamb can identify its mother by her bleat.

When sheep are four years old, they usually have all of their teeth—but no front teeth on top. A bare upper gum and a split in the upper lip enables sheep to graze more closely to the ground than other animals. Sheep spend much of their time eating grass, weeds, and shrubs, often on rocky hillsides and steep slopes that other livestock can not reach. An adult sheep eats 2 to 4½ pounds of food and drinks ½ to 1½ quarts of water per day.

Compared to a Cow . . .

- **Like cows, sheep have four stomach chambers and chew cud (food that they swallow and bring back up into their months to chew and swallow again).**
- **Like cows, sheep can be milked. Sheep's milk has twice the fat of cow's milk and more protein and calcium. Sheep's milk is often used to make fancy cheeses and yogurts.**

(continued)

Baa-lieve It or Not!

- **Sheep fats and fatty acids are the raw material for . . .**

automobile antifreeze	floor wax
candles	herbicides
chewing gum	lotions
chicken feed	margarine
cosmetics	medicines
crayons	paints
dish soaps	shampoos and conditioners
dog food	shaving cream
explosives	tires

- **Sheep bones, horns, and hooves are used to produce . . .**

adhesive tape	ice cream
bandage strips	marshmallows
buttons	photographic film
cellophane wrap and tape	piano keys
combs	syringes
gelatin desserts	toothbrushes
	wallpaper paste

DID YOU KNOW? Some farmers

A sheep's fuzzy fur coat is called a fleece. It keeps the sheep warm through the winter. Once a year, ordinarily in the spring, the fleece is sheared off, usually with electric clippers. Shorn fleece is called raw wool, and, in one year, one sheep can grow about 8 pounds of it. The raw wool is washed to get rid of any dirt, insects, and straw that may have stuck to it, as well as the lanolin, a greasy secretion from the sheep's sebaceous glands. Clean wool is often dyed to a color, combed, and spun into yarn. Wool yarn is used to make sweaters, hats, socks, mittens, and scarves as well as blankets, rugs, and cloth.

Wool is a natural insulator. It can hold up to a third of its weight in moisture without feeling damp. That's why if a wool sweater gets wet from snow or rain, it will still keep you warm.

stralia and Scotland put braces on the teeth of sheep whose teeth grow in crooked so that the animals can eat properly.

Lamb as food is a great source of vitamins and minerals; it is low in fat and full of high-quality protein. The meat from a grown sheep is called mutton, and meat from a sheep less than one year old is called lamb.

1. Where do sheep go to get their hair cut?
2. How do sheep greet each other on December 25?
3. Why did the ram run off the cliff?

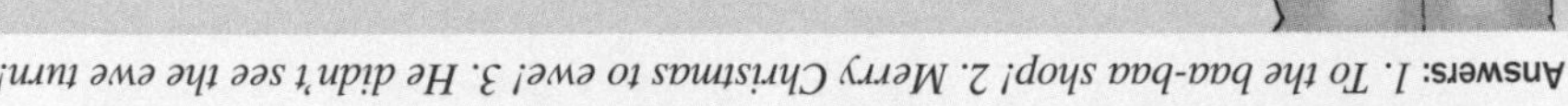

Wild and Woolly FACTS

- Dolly the Sheep, the first cloned mammal, was born on July 5, 1996. She was put to sleep due to lung problems on February 14, 2003.

- **There are about 450 feet of wool yarn in a baseball.**

- Following an oil spill on Phillip Island off southern Australia in January 2000, conservation workers asked knitters around the world to make little wool sweaters for the thousands of Little Penguins that got soaked in oil. (Little Penguins are the world's smallest penguins.) The wool would protect the penguins' feathers and keep them warm after the oil was washed off. More than 10,000 sweaters (more than enough) were knit and sent.

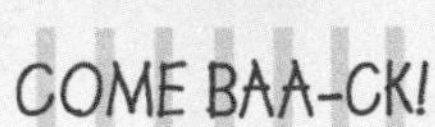

COME BAA-CK!

To hear a sheep bleat, learn about a black sheep, and find more wild and woolly facts, go to **Almanac4kids.com/outdoors.**

HOORAY FOR HORSES

HORSING AROUND

- An adult female horse is a mare.
- An adult male horse is a stallion.
- A young male horse is a colt.
- A young female horse is a filly.
- A horse less than one year old is a foal.
- A full-grown small horse less than 58 inches tall at the withers (shoulders) is a pony.
- The offspring of a donkey and horse is a mule.
- A group of horses is a herd.

What would a farm be without a horse—or two or more? Some farmers depend on horses instead of machines to do much of the hard work on their farms. Not just any horse will do. Draft horses must be used for many tasks because they are bigger and more powerful than saddle horses. Popular breeds of draft horses are Percheron, Belgian, and Clydesdale.

Horses have very good memories and learn by copying what other horses do. That's why a farmer begins training a young draft horse at about age 2 by hitching him to an experienced horse. The two horses work side by side, pulling farm equipment so that the young horse can learn commands such as "start" and "turn." They do this for a couple of years.

CONTINUED

OR
CS?

Once trained, draft horses work in teams. They pull plows, wagons loaded with hay or other crops, hay cutters, and cultivating equipment used to seed fields. Draft teams also pull heavy logs from the woods, collect maple sap for syrup, and give hay- and sleigh rides.

A draft horse weighs about a ton and has hooves the size of dinner plates. It must be groomed, or brushed, every day to keep its coat, mane, and tail clean. The groomer also checks for any small cuts that need treatment and removes debris and small rocks from its hooves. Like our fingernails, horse hooves keep growing and need to be trimmed every few weeks. A farrier removes the horse's shoes, trims its hooves, and fits the horse with new or repaired horseshoes.

A 2,000-pound horse can drink 12 gallons of water and eat up to 60 pounds of hay each day—but not all at once. Horses have small stomachs, so they eat often. Draft horses, which burn a lot of energy, also eat barley, oats, corn, or bran in addition to grass. They love to munch on carrots and apples, too.

DID YOU KNOW?

- **A newborn horse, or foal, can stand up an hour after it's born, and it's able to keep up with the herd within 24 hours.**

Horses have limited eyesight.

They don't see colors clearly; they see many things in shades of gray, and they see things that move best. Objects that are standing still and then suddenly move startle them. A horse's eyes are set on the sides of its head, and it has to move its head to see objects that are next to it, but it can not see behind itself. That's why approaching a horse from behind can be dangerous. The horse might be startled and bite or kick to protect itself. To let a horse know you are near, talk out loud in a soft, friendly voice.

CONTINUED

- **There are about 60 million horses on Earth.**
- **Horses are measured in hands from the ground to the withers, an area between their neck and back. Each hand is four inches. Draft horses stand 16 to 18 hands high.**
- **Horses usually sleep standing up. They lock their back legs into position (sort of like how a kickstand holds up a bicycle). Some horses will stand for a month or more. A horse will lie down to rest only when it feels safe.**

BODY LANGUAGE

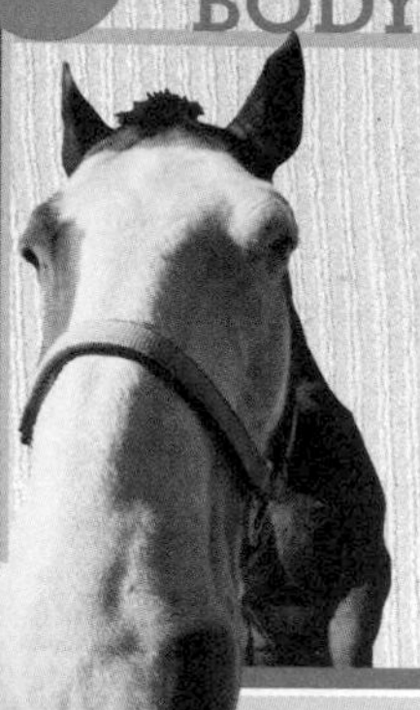

IF A HORSE IS:	YOU WILL SEE:
startled	**a raised head and snorting nostrils**
mad	**ears pinned back**
nervous	**flared nostrils**
happy	**gentle tail swishing**
interested	**ears facing forward and flicking**
relaxed	**ears lowered to the sides slightly**

DID YOU KNOW?

Horses can hear high-pitched tones that humans can't hear! They don't like loud noises, such as machinery or gunshots.

Some people can tell a horse's age by looking at its teeth. They know that a horse is at least five years old if it has its permanent teeth. (These are larger and darker than baby teeth.)

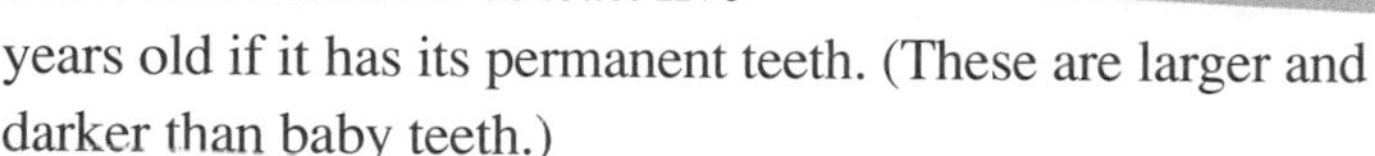

Horses enjoy each other's company. On a farm, two horses will often stand tail to tail, one swatting flies for the other. In the wild, horses roam in herds for safety.

GOOD OL' HORSE SENSE

Can you guess what these horse sayings mean?

1. You can lead a horse to water, but you can't make him drink.
2. Don't put the cart before the horse.
3. Don't change horses in midstream.
4. Don't look a gift horse in the mouth.

ANSWERS: *1. You can show or tell a person how to do something, but you can't force him or her do it. 2. Do first things first. 3. Make a decision and see things through to the end. 4. Appreciate any generosity that comes your way and don't question it.*

FOWL MATTERS

Early American statesman Benjamin Franklin wanted the WILD TURKEY, rather than the bald eagle, to be the national bird of the United States. He thought that the wild turkey was much more respectable and a "bird of courage."

A chicken can RUN at a top speed of 9 MILES PER HOUR. (That's faster than the first roller coaster on New York's Coney Island, built in 1884. It went 6 miles per hour.)

Before modern transportation, farmers in the British Isles put LEATHER SHOES on turkeys and WALKED THEM to market.

To protect a chicken's eyes from pecks by fellow fowl, Andrew Jackson Jr. of Munich, Tennessee, invented TINY SPECTACLES with a headband that allowed them to be placed on a chicken's head and adjusted to fit securely. Andrew was granted a patent for the eye protectors on June 16, 1903.

A male turkey is a TOM and female turkey is a HEN. Both can make a variety of sounds (they can even purr!). Only male turkeys gobble, and that's why they're called GOBBLERS.

What would you call a bird that looks like a cross between a turkey and a chicken? A TURKEN! The Naked Neck chicken breed is also called a Turken because its neck lacks feathers, just as a turkey's does. But a Turken is really all chicken.

A bushel of facts to ponder

During the 1st century B.C., Roman farmers discovered that the best way to grow apples was to cut branches, or scions, from a tree that produced healthy, tasty fruit and graft those branches onto another tree with a strong root. Using this technique, the Romans developed seven different apple varieties from the wild apple.

Early European explorers returning home from foreign lands brought with them unusual fruits and vegetables, such as melons, lemons, oranges, avocados, and eggplants. They called all of these foods "apples" because they didn't know their real names.

CORE LORE

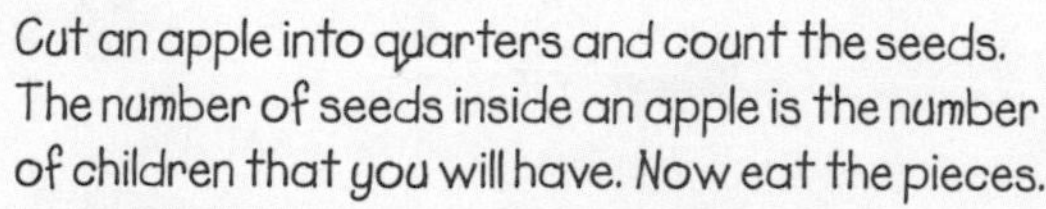

Cut an apple into quarters and count the seeds. The number of seeds inside an apple is the number of children that you will have. Now eat the pieces.

For good health in the coming year, eat an apple on Christmas Eve.

If you cut an apple in half, rub both halves on a wart, and then bury the apple pieces, the wart will disappear.

(Remember, these are just folklore!)

WORD STEMS

- Someone who is loved is sometimes called "the apple of my eye."
- Someone who causes harm is sometimes called a "bad apple."
- Supposedly, the "Adam's apple" (the lump on the front of a man's neck) gets its name from a piece of the apple that Eve gave to Adam in the Garden of Eden, which stuck in his throat, creating a bulge.

In the 1600s, early American colonists called apples "winter bananas" or "melt-in-the-mouths."

According to legend, Johnny Appleseed planted many of the apple orchards in the northeastern United States—but this wasn't his real name. Johnny Appleseed was born John Chapman on September 26, 1774, in Leominster, Massachusetts. As a boy, he worked in an apple orchard, where he learned how to grow apple trees. When he was in his early 20s, he planted his first apple orchard, in Pennsylvania. He later journeyed through Ohio, Michigan, and Indiana, as well as New England, planting apple seeds as he went.

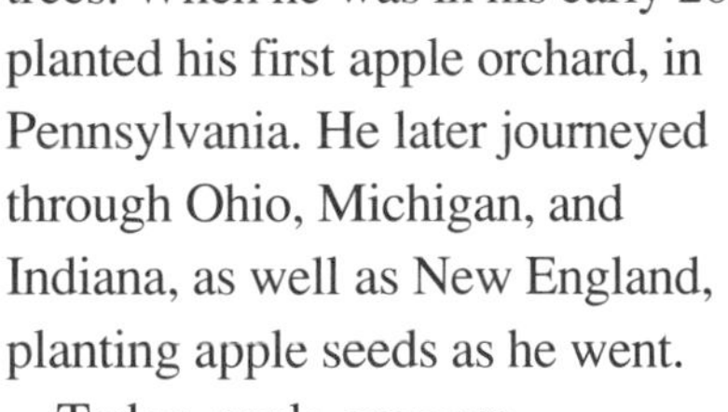

Today, apple growers continue to use the ancient Roman grafting method to produce fruit trees, and there are more than 7,500 apple varieties grown in orchards around the world! About 2,500 apple varieties are grown in North America.

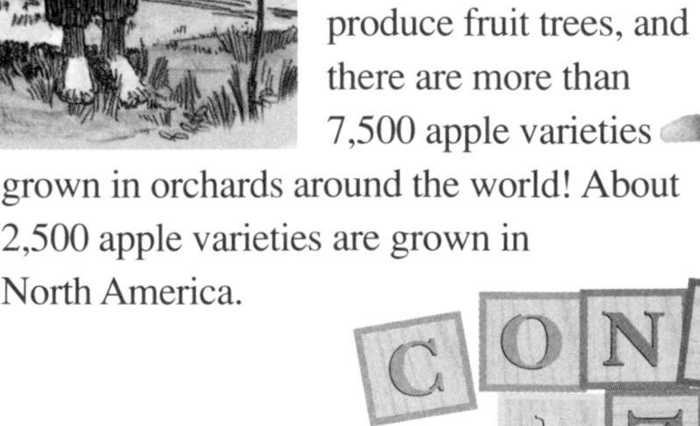

FOOD FOR THOUGHT

The average person eats 50 to 60 apples a year. (That's about 19 pounds!)

Thirsty? EAT AN APPLE. More than 50 percent of the total weight of a fresh apple is water.

It takes about five years for an apple tree with grafted branches to PRODUCE FRUIT.

If **"An apple a day keeps the doctor away,"** are two better for you? Some scientists believe that eating two apples or drinking two glasses of apple juice a day helps to improve your memory and keep your brain sharp. So, the next time you are studying for a big test, munch on an apple—or two.

Feeling claustrophobic, or closed in? SMELL SOME GREEN APPLES. In one experiment, participants claimed that the smell of green apples made an enclosed space seem larger. (The smell of barbecue smoke made the space seem smaller.)

An APPLE PIE contains about two pounds of apples.

One BAD APPLE really can spoil a whole bushel! If an apple is bruised or diseased, it gives off a gas called ethylene, which causes fruits and vegetables to ripen too quickly and thus be more likely to rot. Throw bad apples into the compost pile.

Is It a FRUIT or a VEGETABLE?

Some foods are both!

To a plant expert, or BOTANIST, the part of a flowering plant that bears the seed is the FRUIT. This means that the parts of cucumbers, eggplant, pepper, squash, and watermelon that we eat are very large berries–and thus fruit.

To a culinary expert, or COOK, a plant or part of a plant that is edible and used in food preparation is a VEGETABLE, even if it contains seeds, whereas a FRUIT would be something used as a dessert. Vegetables would include roots (beets and carrots), tubers (potatoes), stems (celery), leaves (lettuce), heads (cauliflower), fruits (tomatoes), and seeds (corn and peas).

To common people, or EVERYBODY ELSE, a vegetable is grown in a kitchen garden and is part of dinner, while a fruit is a dessert.

	TO A BOTANIST	TO A COOK	TO EVERYBODY
Apple	F	F	F
Artichoke	V	V	V
Asparagus	V	V	V
Avocado	F	V	V
Banana	F	F	F
Beet	V	V	V
Broccoli	V	V	V
Brussels sprout	V	V	V
Cabbage	V	V	V
Carrot	V	F*/V	V
Cauliflower	V	V	V
Celery	V	V	V
Corn	F	V	V
Cucumber	F	V	V
Eggplant	F	V	V
Grape	F	F	F
Lettuce	V	V	V
Onion	V	V	V
Parsnip	V	V	V
Pea	F	V	V
Peach	F	F	F
Pear	F	F	F
Pepper	F	V	V
Plum	F	F	F
Potato	V	V	V
Radish	V	V	V
Raspberry	F	F	F
Squash	F	F*/V	V
String bean	F	V	V
Tomato	F	V	V
Watermelon	F	F	F

***Ever heard of CARROT CAKE or SQUASH PIE?**

WEATHER

Meet two of history's most famous—an

The Rain Man

In 1915, southern California was suffering from a drought and the people of San Diego were worried. They needed rain, and they wanted **CHARLES MALLORY HATFIELD** to make it happen.

For years, Charles had conducted experiments and studied weather books, including one called *The Science of Pluviculture,* or rainmaking. He never claimed that he could make rain; he said that he could release rain when the conditions were right. He called himself a "moisture accelerator," but some people called him a "cloud coaxer" and "water magician." He spoke with such confidence that several communities had hired him, so the folks in San Diego did, too.

In December 1915, the Morena dam and reservoir, which held San Diego's water supply, was low, at about one-third full. The city council wanted Charles to fill the reservoir and agreed to pay him $10,000 if he did. Charles and his brother went out to the dam, which was about 60 miles outside of the city, set up camp, and built a 20-foot-tall tower with a platform. They lit a fire and for days boiled a secret mixture of chemicals that evaporated into the air.

Their formula worked—but too well. Rain began on January 10, 1916, but it didn't completely stop for 17 days. Roads flooded, and bridges and railroad tracks were washed away. People died, and thousands of homes were destroyed in what became

WIZARDS

ysterious—meteorological magicians.

known as "Hatfield's Flood." In the end, 28 inches of rain fell! Charles was warned that some people might want revenge. Fearing for their safety, he and his brother took down the tower and fled.

Later, the city council refused to pay the brothers. Charles said that he was sorry, but the damage wasn't their fault. They had done only what they had been asked to do.

We may never know whether Charles brought the rain to San Diego. Prior to his death in 1958, he never discussed his formula with anyone but his brothers and told the public only that he had used 23 chemicals. Today, a plaque at Lake Morena County Park in Campo, California, honors his efforts.

The Ice Man

IRVING LANGMUIR was so curious as a child that he set up his first laboratory in the corner of his bedroom. For him, science was fun. Years later, he became interested in weather while researching ice formation on Mt. Washington in New Hampshire.

One day in 1946, Irving was in his laboratory, in a special freezer built to simulate cloud conditions.

continued

His assistant brought a block of dry ice (frozen carbon dioxide) into the freezer to try to lower the temperature. Suddenly, a small snowstorm began! They discovered that adding dry ice to cold clouds turns the clouds' water vapor into ice and rain.

Irving believed that he could use this discovery not only to make rain but also to change the paths of hurricanes and affect weather patterns. Many people got excited about it, including the U.S. government, and nearly 200 experiments were conducted.

Unfortunately, Irving's technique seems to work only in special, limited situations—like his laboratory.

IDEAS That Are ALL WET

- In ancient times, some people believed that bad smells—such as those from dead bodies after a battle—caused rain. Others believed that explosions from weapons and the like were to blame. A man named Edward Powers wrote in his book, *War and the Weather,* that many Civil War battles produced rain.

- Some people thought that heat—such as fires—produced rain. In the 1850s, a meteorologist named James Espy even suggested that rain could be made by starting huge forest fires.

A RECIPE FOR RAIN . . .

Today, airplanes are used to "make rain" by seeding, or sprinkling, clouds with dry ice or chemicals such as silver iodide, which has a chemical structure close to that of ice. However, nobody can prove that cloud seeding is widely effective and worth the expense. One problem is that it is hard to tell whether seeding produced rain or a cloud was simply ready to produce rain by itself.

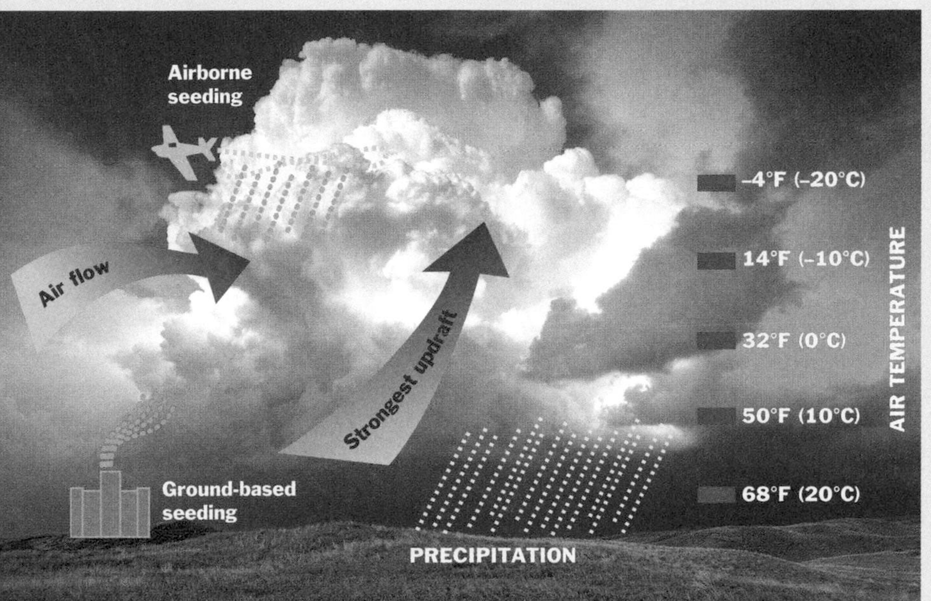

TIROS Meteorological Satellite

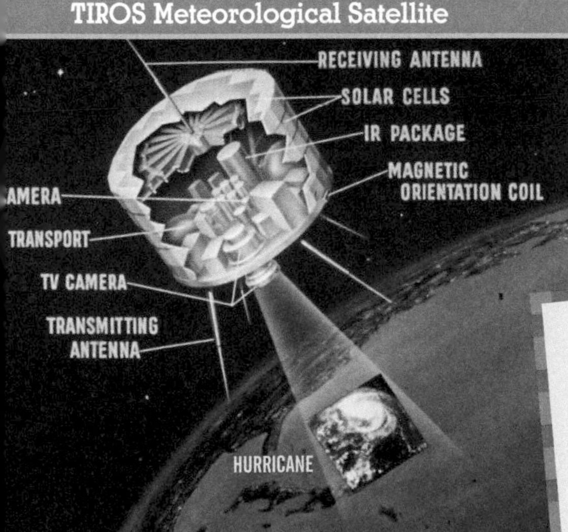

Modern scientists are using radar and satellites to study clouds more closely to determine once and for all how well cloud seeding really works.

WHAT'S THE WEATHER GOING TO BE?

Sun? Rain? Snow? Find out what to expect right over your head at **Almanac4kids.com/weather.**

BEWARE OF BLACK BLIZZARDS

This is not about sooty snow. A black blizzard is another name for a dust storm, one of the most terrifying and destructive weather events.

DUST STORMS can occur when certain conditions exist:

- prolonged drought
- high temperatures
- overcultivated, mismanaged, or excessively grazed soil

THE DIRTY THIRTIES

Some of the worst dust storms in history occurred in the Great Plains region of the United States and Canada in the 1930s. Carried on fierce, howling winds, clouds of dust miles wide and thousands of feet high swept across the region for hours or even days at a time. The blinding storms blocked the Sun and turned day into night, which caused some hens to roost but not lay any eggs. The winds blew corn off stalks, bricks out of chimneys, and shingles off roofs. Gusts toppled windmills, barns, and outbuildings. Dust piled up on roads, making driving impossible. Grit gummed up motors, stopping cars and buses in their tracks, and drifted over fences, allowing cattle and horses to walk over them and wander away. Dust penetrated the tiniest crevices in windows and doors, coating food, dishes, curtains, floors, and furnishings. It blinded cattle and suffocated them

DARK DAYS

On May 11, 1934, dust from a storm that had originated in the Great Plains darkened the skies over Washington, D.C., and New York City, before blowing 300 miles out over the Atlantic, where it fell onto the decks of ships.

April 14, 1935, the day of the worst black blizzard, came to be known as Black Sunday.

On April 15, 1935, a newspaper reporter introduced the term "Dust Bowl" to refer to the U.S. Great Plains.

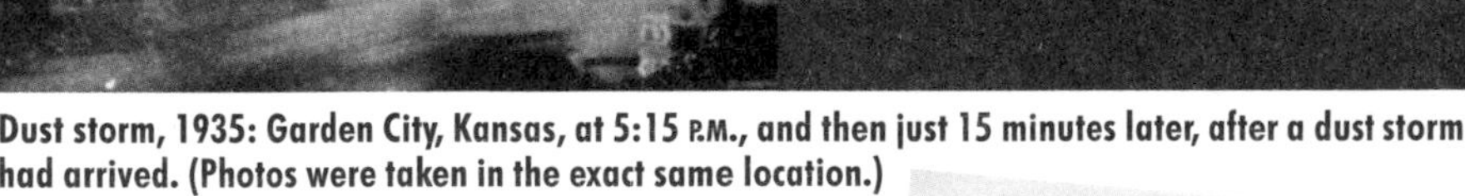

Dust storm, 1935: Garden City, Kansas, at 5:15 P.M., and then just 15 minutes later, after a dust storm had arrived. (Photos were taken in the exact same location.)

when the dust they breathed in turned to mud in their lungs. Dust buried small animals such as rabbits, birds, and mice.

In autumn of 1939, rain finally fell, and farmers eventually returned to their fields. They used new techniques to keep the topsoil from eroding and to ensure that black blizzards would not return. They seeded areas with grass, began rotating crops, adopted contour- and strip-plowing methods, and planted trees in rows to break the winds that swept across the plains.

CONTINUED

Count 'Em

It is impossible to know exactly how many black blizzards rolled across the U.S. Great Plains, but estimates have been made about storms that struck large areas (all or parts of several states).

YEAR	NUMBER OF WIDE-RANGING DUST STORMS
1932	14
1933	38
1934	22
1935	40
1936	68
1937	72
1938	61
1939	30

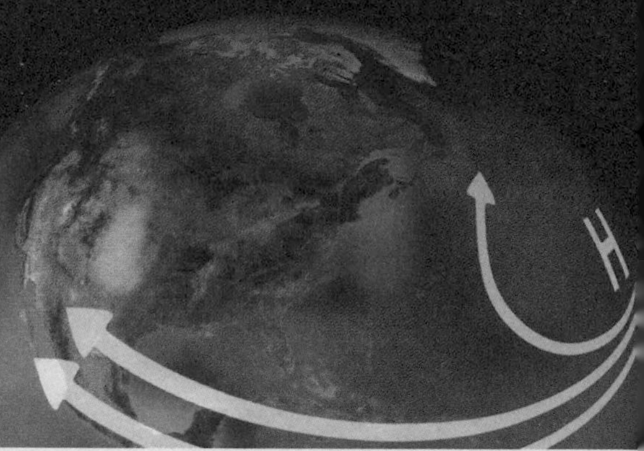

Global weather patterns contributed to the 1930s drought. A low-level jet stream, a ribbon of fast-moving air near Earth's surface, normally flows westward over the Gulf of Mexico and then northward, during the summer, pulling up moisture and dumping rain onto the Great Plains. In the 1930s, this jet stream weakened and traveled farther south than normal *(above)*.

When the Dust Settled . . .

Scientists believe that some of the dust particles in ice core samples retrieved from Greenland in 2003 may have come from the U.S. Great Plains during the 1930s.

Blowing Through Time

The Dust Bowl period was neither the beginning nor the end of black blizzards and their effects.

According to a newspaper report in Wichita, Kansas, in the 1880s, dust storms were so bad that dust, grit, and sand were in people's food, up their noses, down their backs, and between their toes. When people were outside, the only way they could communicate was through hand signals. In order to talk, they would go to a room without any windows or cracks, pull out their earplugs, and wash out their mouths before speaking.

In 2004, it was estimated that up to 3 billion tons of dust is blown around the world annually.

The use of four-wheel-drive vehicles instead of camels to travel in deserts is believed to have increased the amount of dust in the air.

Occasionally, when African dust storms blow across the Atlantic, swarms of large grasshoppers get caught up in them and make it all the way to the Caribbean—alive.

NASA scientists use satellites to track dust storms around the world.

Above: **A massive dust cloud swirls around the north pole on Mars.** ***Below:*** **A similar dust cloud on Earth blows westward from the Sahara Desert.**

OTHERWORLDLY WEATHER

The only other planet known to have dust storms is Mars. There, they can last for weeks or even months!

- In 1971, the biggest Martian dust storm ever recorded covered the entire planet, obscuring it for weeks from the view of *Mariner 9*, the first spacecraft to reach it.
- Martian dust storms grow to be larger than those on Earth because the surface of the red planet is like a desert, with no liquid water.
- Dust grains in dust storms on Mars are tiny—as fine as the particles in smoke.

FOOD FLOODS!

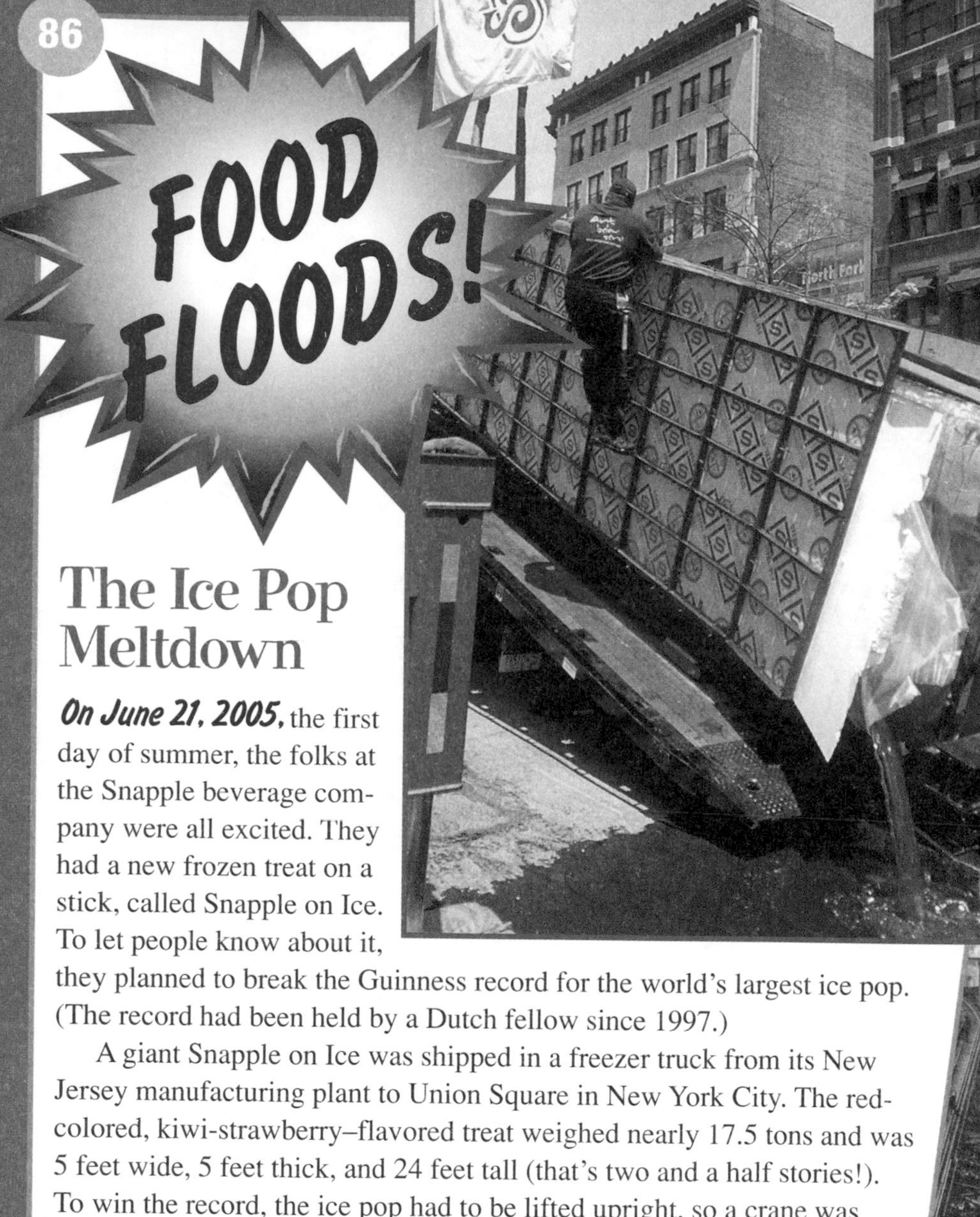

The Ice Pop Meltdown

On June 21, 2005, the first day of summer, the folks at the Snapple beverage company were all excited. They had a new frozen treat on a stick, called Snapple on Ice. To let people know about it, they planned to break the Guinness record for the world's largest ice pop. (The record had been held by a Dutch fellow since 1997.)

A giant Snapple on Ice was shipped in a freezer truck from its New Jersey manufacturing plant to Union Square in New York City. The red-colored, kiwi-strawberry–flavored treat weighed nearly 17.5 tons and was 5 feet wide, 5 feet thick, and 24 feet tall (that's two and a half stories!). To win the record, the ice pop had to be lifted upright, so a crane was there to raise it. An official Guinness judge was waiting to inspect.

The weather that day was 82°F—too warm, as it turned out. The crane began to lift the ice pop, but then it stopped and held the ice pop at an angle. The giant Snapple on Ice was melting! It was turning to slush and then to little rivers of red juice that poured onto the street. Officials decided that it was too dangerous to continue. They were afraid that the ice pop might collapse, splashing onto the street and everyone who had gathered to watch. The crane lowered it to safety.

Soon, fire trucks appeared and police closed off a few streets. They thought that cars, bicyclists, and pedestrians might slip. The Breaking News Network reported that there was "sticky goo all over the area." Finally, the giant red slush-on-a-stick was carted back to New Jersey without breaking a record, and firemen hosed down the streets.

FROZEN IN TIME

The record for the largest ice pop belongs to Jan van den Berg and friends, of The Netherlands. On August 30, 1997, they made a giant frozen Rocket that weighed more than 10 tons. It was 21 feet tall, 7½ feet wide, and 3 feet 7 inches thick, on average. The temperature there on that day was about 60°F.

A Sea of Molasses

A big, sticky mess once covered the streets of Boston.

For years, molasses had been used to sweeten cakes, cookies, and breads, and to make baked beans and rum. Boston was considered the molasses capital of the nation. More molasses was processed there than in any other U.S. city, and molasses factories, warehouses, and storage tanks lined the harbor. One of the biggest tanks was 58 feet tall and 90 feet in diameter; it held about 2.5 million gallons of gooey brown molasses.

continued

On January 15, 1919, Boston was unusually warm. At noon, the temperature was 43°F. Kids played in the streets. Workers came out of the factories for lunch. Mothers hung laundry out to dry.

Suddenly, a loud roar was heard. The huge tank had broken open! Molasses exploded into the sky like a geyser, and 14,000 tons of it poured out onto the streets. It wasn't just stinky and messy; it was dangerous. A 15-foot-high wave picked up a boy and carried him several blocks like a surfer. People were sure he was dead, but he survived. Others were not so lucky: 21 people died and more than 50 were hurt. The molasses buried horses, destroyed buildings, and knocked down elevated train tracks. Rescue workers rushed to the scene, but they and their equipment got stuck in the muck. The next day, firemen hosed the area with salt water because it cut through the stickiness better than fresh water.

Many people believe that the explosion was due to the warm weather, but in fact we may never really know what caused it.

STINKY FOR YEARS

Molasses is a thick syrup that comes from sugarcane that has been harvested, mashed, and boiled as many as three times. Each boil results in a darker, more bitter molasses. Years after the molasses flood, people in Boston continued to claim that the neighborhood near the explosion smelled sweet—just like molasses.

The Great Pumpkin Flood

People often pull pranks at Halloween, but the Great Pumpkin Flood of 1786 was no laughing matter.

On October 5 that year, heavy rains caused the Delaware and Susquehanna rivers to run over their banks in Pennsylvania. The rising water pulled pumpkins off their vines, and the current carried them away. One person noted: "Heavy pumpkins came tumbling downstream like great orange cannonballs." The pumpkins acted like cannonballs, too, the observer added, when they hit people or houses.

Weather Phobias

Weather Condition	Name(s) of Fear
Clouds	Nephophobia
Cold	Cheimatophobia Frigophobia Psychrophobia
Dampness, moisture	Hygrophobia
Daylight, sunshine	Heliophobia Phengophobia
Extreme cold, frost, ice	Cryophobia Pagophobia
Floods	Antlophobia
Fog	Homichlophobia Nebulaphobia
Heat	Thermophobia
Hurricanes, tornadoes	Lilapsophobia
Lightning, thunder	Astraphobia Brontophobia Keraunophobia
Northern lights, southern lights	Auroraphobia
Rain	Ombrophobia Pluviophobia
Snow	Chionophobia
Thunder	Ceraunophobia Tonitrophobia
Wind	Ancraophobia Anemophobia

THE WORLD'S Fuzziest

Years ago, before satellites and radar, people began using plants and animals to predict the weather. One of the most famous of these prognosticators is probably the woolly bear, also called the woolly worm. But this fuzzy forecaster is neither a bear nor a worm—it is a caterpillar! And it does not feel soft like wool; it feels stiff like bristles.

Forecaster

Like many other caterpillars, the woolly bear hatches from a moth egg during warm weather. During spring and summer, it snacks on dandelions, asters, clover, tree leaves, and other vegetation. When the weather turns cool, it looks for shelter under bark or inside logs where it can spend the winter. This is when the woolly bear's forecasting formula is at its peak! Watch for woolly bears crawling across streets and sidewalks. Pick one up, and carefully study the black and brown stripes of its coat.

According to weather folklore . . .

- If a woolly bear's brown stripe is wide, the winter will be mild. If the brown band is narrow, the winter will be cold and harsh.
- If its front black section is wide, the winter will start with several weeks of cold weather. If its back black section is wide, the winter will end with weeks of cold weather.

Put the woolly bear back on the ground so that it can find a winter home. The next spring, it will make a cocoon, pupate into its adult form (the Isabella tiger moth), and fly away!

SIGNS OF CHANGE

Look and listen for other natural weather forecasters:

If TOADS hurry toward water, it is going to thunder.

When COWS bellow in the evening, expect snow that night.

When SWALLOWS fly in circles, expect rain.

If ANTS their walls do frequent build, rain will from the clouds be spilled.

When the PEACOCK loudly bawls, soon we'll have both rain and squalls.

By the Sea, by the Sea, by the BEAUTIFUL SEA...

When a wave travels through the ocean, very little water really moves to a new location. Think of what happens when you jerk a rope quickly up and down one time. You create a wave. Energy, in the form of the wave or ripple, travels in the rope, but the ends of the rope do not move much from their original position after the wave has passed.

Ocean waves can be caused by wind, gravity, and underwater disturbances, and they can start from halfway around the world.

The wind can form everything from tiny ripples to towering cliffs of water on the surface of the ocean, depending on the wind's speed and how long and far it blows.

The pull of gravity from the Moon (and to a lesser degree, the Sun) causes Earth's tides, when combined with

Q. What did the beach say when the tide came in?

A. Long time, no sea.

There's LOTS FOR YOU TO DO at the beach—and there's LOTS GOING ON. Plants, animals, weather, rocks, and even the Sun and Moon all play a part in the ever-changing seashore environment.

TAKE A LOOK!

the force created by Earth's rotation (called centrifugal force). In many places, there are about 12½ hours between one high tide and the next (and between one low tide and the next). Each cycle from high tide to high tide is actually the passing of two giant bulges of water caused by gravity.

Underwater earthquakes, volcanic eruptions, or landslides can also create waves, by pushing water away from the disturbed area. Tsunamis can sometimes result from these events. A tsunami is a series of fast-moving waves that increase in height as they approach shore, often causing much destruction along the coastline.

Many beaches have **seaweeds.** They come in a variety of shapes, including flat, stringy, feathery, or ruffly. Most are simple forms of plant life called algae.

CONTINUED

GREEN ALGAE are commonly found in areas that are exposed when the tide goes out (called the intertidal zone) and in shallow water.

BROWN ALGAE tend to grow larger than other types. Many brown algae, such as rockweeds, are found in the intertidal zone or just below it (subtidal); others, such as kelp, grow in deeper water.

RED ALGAE can live at great depths (down to 650 feet!), since they gather sunlight in semidark waters better than other types of algae.

Don't let the names fool you: Brown algae can also be beige, yellow, or nearly black. Red algae can also be purple, yellow, or orange.

Some seaweeds live in free-floating masses on top of the water, but most attach themselves to rocks by anchors called holdfasts. Some seaweeds have gas-filled bladders that allow their leaflike blades to float near the surface. The largest seaweeds can grow to more than 195 feet long!

How about a double scoop of brown kelp?

Seaweeds are found in many products, including:
- soaps
- toothpastes
- fertilizers
- health food

and even
- ICE CREAM!

Beach sand is made from rocks (such as quartz) or animal remains (such as coral or shells) that were broken into tiny bits by ocean waves or were eroded elsewhere and then carried to the shore by inland streams or ocean currents. Sand can be many colors: white, tan, pink, red, green, or black.

Some sea creatures develop **shells** to protect themselves. Others, such as hermit crabs, live in discarded shells. Univalves, such as whelks, conches,

and periwinkles, have just one shell. Bivalves, such as clams and scallops, have two shells held together by strong muscles.

Starfish are living creatures! (Remember that when you see dried ones in gift shops or at friends' homes.) A starfish has a mouth in the center of its underside, and, depending on what type it is, it may have five arms or more than 20! (If a starfish loses an arm, it grows a new one.) Each arm has hundreds of tiny tube feet that help the starfish to move and to capture food. Many starfish eat clams, oysters, and similar sea animals, using their tube feet to pry apart the shells.

Sandy, Salty, SEASIDE SAYINGS

Twist your tongue around these maritime maddeners by trying to say them three times in a row:

She saw a fish on the seashore and I'm sure the fish she saw on the seashore was a sawfish.

Six slippery snails slid slowly seaward.

Selfish shellfish.

And, of course . . .

She sells seashells by the seashore.

MAKE A GOURD • BIRD

YOU WILL NEED:

- round or curlicue-shape gourd, completely dried
- 12-inch ruler
- drill or sharp knife
- round stick or wooden dowel for perch, about ¼-inch in diameter
- weatherproof cord or string

In colonial days, Native Americans hung dried, hollowed-out gourds to attract birds to their villages. It's an idea that still works.

Choose a gourd that is large enough for a bird to live in, but not too large to hang from a tree branch. To dry it, keep it in a warm area with

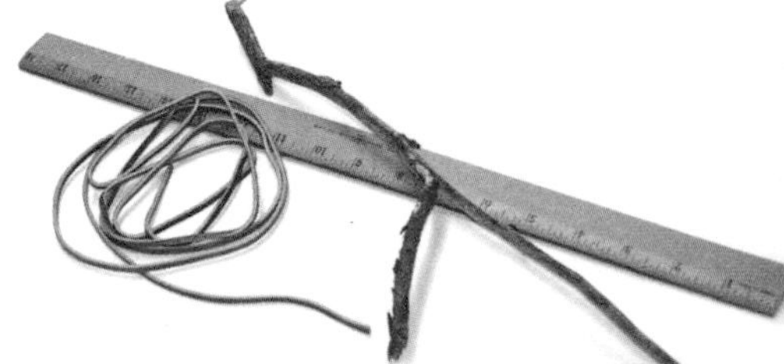

HOUSE

SIZE IT RIGHT

Small birds, such as wrens, need a house that is about 4 inches wide, with a 1½-inch-wide entrance. Bigger birds, like purple martins, need a house about 6 inches wide, with a 2½-inch-wide entrance.

good air circulation (this may take several months). When the seeds rattle and tapping it produces a hollow sound, it's ready.

Making a gourd birdhouse is fun and easy but, if necessary, ask an adult to help you.

Using a drill or sharp knife, make the entrance hole at least one-third of the way up from the bottom of the large part of the gourd. Half an inch below the entrance hole, drill or cut a small hole the diameter of your stick or dowel perch and put the perch into the hole.

Make two or three small holes in the bottom of the gourd for drainage and two holes in the top for the cord hanger. Run a piece of cord through the holes in the top. Leave enough length to hang and tie it.

In the spring, hang the birdhouse on a branch where you can see it. To attract many birds, make a few birdhouses and place them on neighboring trees.

FAST-FOOD FOR FEATHERED FRIENDS

Even birds get snack attacks. Try these quick ways to welcome birds to your yard:

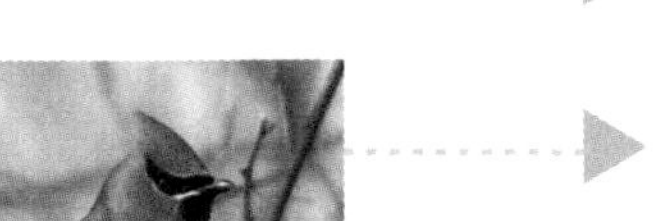

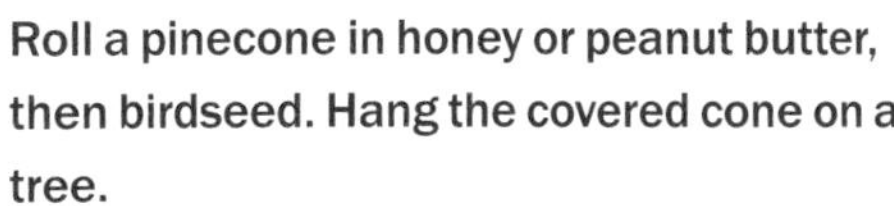

- Hang stale doughnuts and bagels on a tree. (Woodpeckers love them!)
- Roll a pinecone in honey or peanut butter, then birdseed. Hang the covered cone on a tree.
- Put your old Christmas tree outside and decorate it with strung peanuts in their shells, popcorn, or cranberries.

CREEPY, CRAWLY, Coming AT YOU!

SPIDERS ARE ARACHNIDS.

Arachnids are animals with eight legs (four pairs), no antennae, no wings, and only two body parts. The arachnid group also includes scorpions, mites, and ticks.

Spiders live almost everywhere: on the ground, on plants, in tree branches, among grasses, under rocks, and on water.

Most spiders are either wanderers or web builders. Wanderers usually hunt on land, ambushing their prey. Web builders catch their food in webs.

All spiders spin silk, and each kind of silk has its own purpose:

- **sticky silk, for catching insects**
- **web frame silk, which gives a spiderweb its structure**
- **egg sac silk, for wrapping the babies**

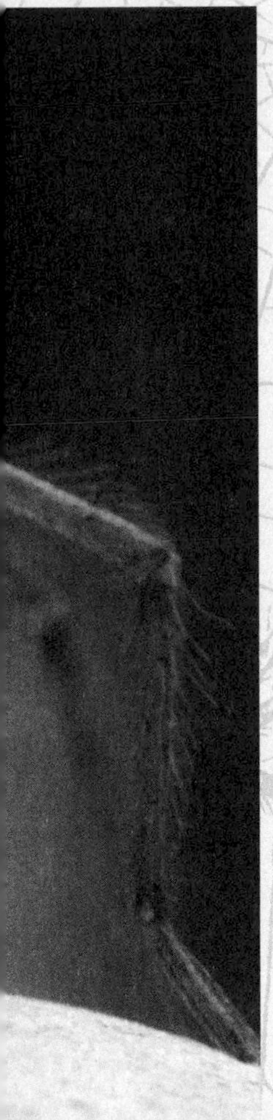

Spiderwebs can be shaped like funnels, bowls, domes, sheets, and orbs, depending on the spider type. Spiders don't stick to their own webs because they don't walk on the sticky parts. (Also, some spiders have oil on their bodies.)

Spiderweb silk is very strong. Scientists, the military, and the medical industry have tried (and so far failed) to duplicate spider silk. They have also tried to raise spiders that would make silk, but spiders raised together tend to eat each other.

Orb spider webs are some of the most familiar. They are woven in open areas between plant stems or tree branches. Each orb spider species, or type, has its own web pattern. When the orb spider rebuilds its web, usually in the same spot, it eats the old web silk as it goes. (The silk contains protein.) Building a new web takes an orb spider about an hour.

continued

Most spiders don't see very well, even though they may have as many as eight eyes. Instead, they identify insects and intruders that touch their web by the vibrations that they make. Spiderwebs trap 95 percent of the insects that touch them.

Once an insect is caught, the spider stabs it with hollow, daggerlike fangs and kills or paralyzes it with an injection of powerful venom, or poison. The spider then pumps digestive fluid into the insect's body and sucks out its juices.

An Itsy-Bitsy SUPERSTITION

A spider crawling on your clothes is a sign of good luck.

WEE ONES, AW-A-A-A-Y!

Depending on the species, spiders may produce from two to 3,000 eggs. Each egg group is covered with a strong silk covering, or egg sac. When many young spiders, or spiderlings, are ready to leave home, they climb onto a fence post, tree branch, or high blade of grass. Each gives off a silken thread. As the silk thread gets longer, wind carries the spiderling away. This is called spider "ballooning." Baby spiders will weave the same type of web as their parents, only a lot smaller.

An Itsy-Bitsy SUPERSTITION

A spider in your pocket means that you will soon get money.

An Itsy-Bitsy SUPERSTITION

Find a spiderweb with your initials in it near your front door, and you will be lucky forever.

EYES SPY SPIDERS

Scientists have counted about 37,000 different kinds of spiders. Here are a few:

- **trap-door spiders**
- **purse-web spiders**
- **ogre-faced spiders**
- **jumping spiders**
- **spitting spiders**
- **wolf spiders**
- **fishing spiders**

There are also spiders that resemble ants, tree bark, and bird poop on a leaf.

GOING BATTY

For centuries, people have said that bats are evil and dangerous. YOU DECIDE.

Bats are social animals, and it is common for them to roost or sleep together in large groups called colonies. Bats are attracted to dark or semidark places, such as caves, under bridges, or abandoned buildings. Some tropical varieties hang out in treetops. Often, a colony will adopt an orphaned bat, and some bats will even regurgitate (throw up!) their food to share it with their less well-fed cavemates.

Most bats hunt at night. They navigate in the dark by making high-pitched noises with their nose or mouth. (Humans are unable to hear bat calls.) When the sound bounces back from objects such as trees or houses, bats are able to form pictures in their brains of what is in front of and around them. This process is called echolocation; it is used by most bats to identify objects they should avoid. It also tells them where their next meal, such as a large swarm of mosquitoes, is located.

White-winged vampire bats

When bats roost, they hang upside down by their toes and wrap their wings around themselves. Their toes have claws that they use to hold on to their perch, and their knees are rotated 180 degrees. Their wings are like four long fingers connected with a covering of very thin skin. Bats also have a "thumb," which they sometimes use to grasp bugs or other small prey.

[CONTINUED]

Little red flying fox bats

Like humans, bats usually give birth to only one baby at a time. Bat pups are usually born in the spring. They feed on their mother's milk for about a month, until they are able to fly and hunt on their own. The pups do not have any fur when they are born, and their skin is pink. Although they look helpless, they have strong legs and sharp claws, which they use to hold on to their mother when she is roosting. The average life expectancy of most bats is about 30 years (that's equal to a human life expectancy of about 100 human years).

DID YOU KNOW?

Bat guano (poop) is collected and used to fertilize crops. It is also used in making some products such as laundry detergent.

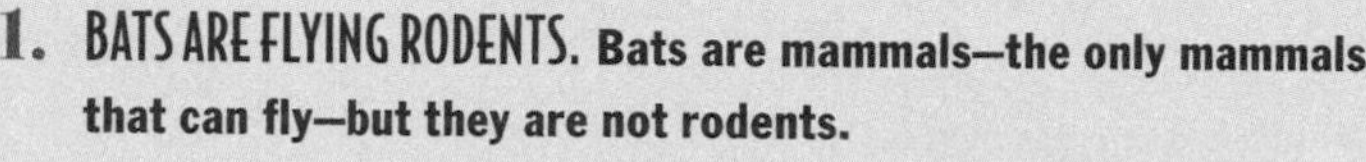

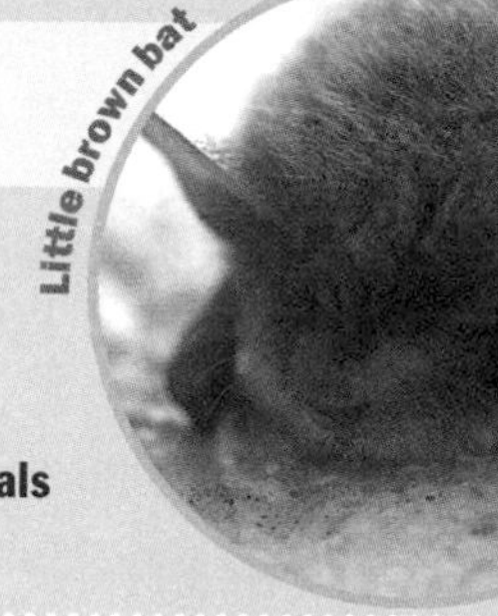

Little brown bat

1. **BATS ARE FLYING RODENTS.** **Bats are mammals—the only mammals that can fly—but they are not rodents.**
2. **BATS ARE BLIND.** **"Blind as a bat" is an expression that creates a false impression. Bats are not blind. They see better during the nighttime but see only in black and white, like many other animals.**
3. **ALL BATS CARRY RABIES.** **Bats are no more likely to carry rabies than any other wild animal. In the United States, rabid bats are the cause of just one death per year, on average. Worldwide, rabid dogs account for 99 percent of the deaths due to rabies.**
4. **BATS WILL SWOOP DOWN AND GET CAUGHT IN YOUR HAIR.** **Only in the movies. They swoop in flight not to attack, but because their wings are structured differently than birds' wings. Bats are afraid of humans and just want to be left alone to hunt for food, feed their young, and sleep.**
5. **BATS ARE DIRTY.** **Bats are cleaner than many kids! When they return to their roost, bats will often spend as much as 30 minutes cleaning themselves—and often their cavemates, too—before they settle down to sleep.**

BAT STATS

There are more than 1,000 species of bats in the world. Here are a few . . .

Flying fox bats are found in Australia, Africa, Asia, and the South Pacific islands. One species is the largest bat in the world, with a wingspan of nearly 6 feet.

Fruit bat

Fruit bats can be found in Africa, India, and Southeast Asia. Their strong sense of smell guides them to their preferred dinner—ripe fruit.

The **bumblebee bat,** found in Thailand, is about the size of a jelly bean and weighs less than a penny.

Bumblebee bat

Little brown bats are common in North America. Adults weigh about ½ ounce, and they consume about half their body weight each day in small insects that they catch and eat in midair.

In Latin America, the **common vampire bat** sips blood from sleeping horses, cattle, and other large animals. It uses its two razor-sharp front teeth to prick its host animal—usually in the feet, nose, or ear tips—and then laps up the blood, about 2 tablespoons per feeding.

The **western mastiff,** which weighs approximately 2 ounces, is the largest type of bat found in the United States.

Do not attempt to handle bats yourself. The person in the photo above is a trained professional. If you find a bat on the ground, please call Bat Conservation International at 512-327-9721.

Common vampire bat

Western mastiff bat

MAKE A TOAD ABODE

Toads will camp out wherever they find insects, but they prefer cool, wet places. (They do not like yards or gardens that have been treated with pesticides.) To encourage a toad to move into your yard, give it a home.

YOU WILL NEED:

- a garden shovel
- sand
- a few rocks
- a small board
- a pie plate
- water

Find a spot under a shady plant. Dig a hole about 10 inches wide by 3 inches deep. Spread a layer of sand in it. Place rocks around the hole, leaving a toad-size entry. Lay a large, flat rock or board across the rocks.

Toads are natural bug zappers. A toad's zapper is its long tongue, which is attached at the front of the lower jaw, with the tip pointing back into its throat. When a toad spies an insect, the toad whips out its entire tongue, trapping the victim on the sticky tip, and then withdraws its tongue and deposits the insect into its throat. All this happens faster than the human eye can follow.

Toads catch and eat many of the bugs that destroy garden plants—cutworms, caterpillars, grubs, and squash bugs, to name a few. Toads also eat bugs that annoy gardeners. One toad will gobble up nearly 10,000 pesky insects, including mosquitoes, in one summer.

When a toad (or its cousin, the frog) swallows, it looks like it is blinking. Its eyes sink down through its skull and press on the roof of its mouth to help push food down its throat.

IT EATS ITS OWN SKIN!

A well-fed toad grows so fast that its skin becomes too small, so it sheds that skin as often as every three to ten days in warm weather. When the old skin splits up its back, the toad pulls the skin off with its mouth and feet, rolling it into a ball. (New skin is in place.) Then the toad eats its old skin, which it considers a nutritious snack.

To make a pool for your toad, scoop a hole in the ground that is the size of the pie plate. Make sure that the edge of the plate is level with the ground. Set the plate in the hole and fill the plate with water.

Be patient. A toad may eventually discover your toad abode. If you make other toad houses, scatter them throughout the yard. A toad usually likes to be the only one in its territory.

MEET THE WINTER WARRIORS

Animals hav

All animals need energy to live, and they get it by digesting food. During winter, food is hard to find, so some creatures cope by becoming less active. This reduces their need for energy, which reduces their need for food. Many mammals take this one step further and hibernate. Hibernation is a state of inactivity and sleep. The animal's body temperature drops to near freezing for a long time, and its rate of metabolism (the ways it makes and uses energy) slows way down. There are several kinds of hibernators.

Some squirrels and mice are **true hibernators.** The body temperatures of true hibernators can drop to as low as 36°F.

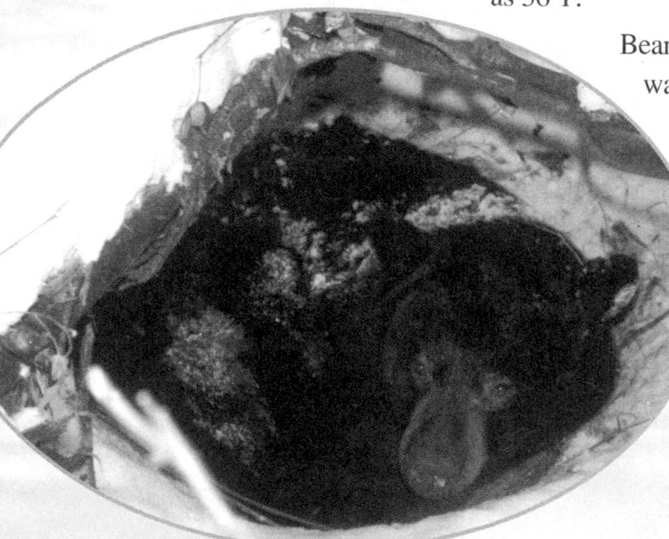

Bears are **nappers.** They wake up to move around a little but not to eat. They rely on fat stored in their bodies as their source of energy. Body temperatures of 59°F or less can be fatal to nappers.

fferent ways of surviving frigid conditions.

Raccoons and skunks are **nappers and snackers.** They store food before winter, hibernate, and wake periodically to snack. Their body temperatures drop while they are napping and rise after they wake up.

The wood frog and some of its close relatives, including the spring peeper, are **cold keepers.** They hibernate under just a few leaves below the snow. When temperatures outside fall below freezing, the frog's liver secretes extra glucose, or blood sugar—as much as 100 times the normal level. The glucose travels through the bloodstream to organs, where it acts like the antifreeze in a car. This enables the frog to withstand temperatures down to about 20°F. During this time, the frog's heart stops beating, breathing comes to a halt, and the frog feels like an ice cube.

Like a frog, a snake is "cold-blooded" and can't produce enough heat to keep its body temperature above that of the surrounding environment. To avoid freezing in winter, a snake goes underground and curls up into a ball, called a solitary huddle. It can save even more heat by forming a larger ball with other snakes. That's why snakes are known as **group huddlers.**

CONTINUED

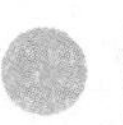

Pass the fat, please

The important blood vessels and organs of hibernating mammals are surrounded by a special **brown fat.** When an animal begins to awaken from hibernation, brown fat generates heat that the blood carries throughout the body, allowing the animal to warm up quickly, without shivering. Once the animal is fully awake, its body temperature returns to normal—and if it gets a chill, it will shiver naturally.

You had brown fat when you were an infant. It helped keep you warm without shivering, too.

NO HIBERNATORS HERE

Some insects remain active over the winter. Honeybees stay warm by clustering in their hives and repeatedly contracting their wing muscles without moving their wings. All this activity keeps the outer layers of bees above 57°F and the inner core up at around 90°F. (To expend this much energy, the bees eat lots of stored honey.) The outer layers of bees change places with the inner ones every so often so that none of them get too cold.

Some insects, such as ants and termites, go into the soil, well below the frost level, to avoid freezing in winter.

Birds have many ways of coping with winter. For example, lots of birds shiver. During shivering, muscles contract and release rapidly, which creates body heat.

HOW COLD IS IT WHERE YOU ARE? Go to **Almanac4kids.com/weather** and see what the weather will be tonight!

In addition, birds fluff their feathers to create air pockets close to the skin, increasing insulation. Ruffled feathers help to trap body heat, including the heat created by shivering.

Tracker's Guide

Keep an eye out for signs of these animals. Their tracks can often be found as close as your own backyard.

RED SQUIRREL

Habitat: Coniferous and deciduous forests; wooded parks
Weight: 8 to 12 ounces
Length: 11 to 14 inches, including a 4- to 5-inch tail
Diet: Berries, birds' eggs, fruit, mushrooms and other fungi, nuts, seeds
Territory: Northern United States; Rocky Mountains south to Arizona and New Mexico; Canada

COMMON RACCOON

Habitat: Woodlands, grasslands, farmland, suburbs—especially if water is nearby
Weight: Males, 15 to 30 pounds; females, 10 to 20 pounds
Height: 9 to 12 inches at shoulder
Length: 26 to 42 inches, including an 8- to 14-inch tail
Diet: Berries, birds' eggs, cat food, corn, fish, frogs, garbage, insects, mice, nuts, salamanders, shellfish
Territory: Throughout North America

EASTERN CHIPMUNK

Habitat: Deciduous forests, fallen logs, suburban and rural yards, city parks
Weight: 3 to 6 ounces
Length: 8 to 11 inches, including a 3- to 4-inch tail
Diet: Berries, grain, insects, nuts, seeds, slugs, small snakes, snails, worms
Territory: Eastern and central United States; eastern Canada

The Shortcut That Wasn't

On April 14, 1846, about 90 pioneers—families mostly, with children of all ages—from Springfield, Illinois, began their journey west by wagon train to settle in California. Led by brothers George and Jacob Donner and James Frazier Reed, this ill-fated group is now famously known as the **Donner Party.**

Jacob brought with him *The Emigrants' Guide to Oregon and California* by Lansford W. Hastings. The author claimed that a shortcut, later known as the Hastings Cutoff, would cut nearly 400 miles off the trip and save time. He didn't reveal that he had never traveled it.

OREGON TRAIL
Donner Lake
CALIFORNIA TRAIL
Great Salt Lake
Hastings Cutoff
SUTTER'S FORT
Springfield

{continued}

By late June, the pioneers had reached Wyoming, where they met James Clyman, who had just traveled the cutoff in reverse. He warned the pioneers that the cutoff was "the most desolate country" in the world. "Take the regular wagon track and never leave it," he advised.

James Reed was in a hurry. He wanted to cross the Sierra Nevada Mountains before winter, so on July 31, the group started into the cutoff. Because the pioneers had to clear the road for their wagons, the trip was more difficult and took longer than expected.

Almost a month later, they reached the Great Salt Lake and the barren Salt Lake Desert. According to the guidebook, the desert was 40 miles across. In fact, it was 80 miles wide. It took five days to cross. It was not until late September that the weary group rejoined the main trail in eastern Nevada. The shortcut turned out to have been 125 miles longer than the regular route—and it cost them dearly. Food supplies had dwindled. One pioneer had abandoned his 60-year-old companion. Native Americans had killed one man and 21 oxen, which meant that wagons had to be left behind. Another man died in a gun accident.

Near the end of October, the travelers thought that their bad luck was behind them when two scouts from a fort at Sacramento, California, arrived with emergency supplies. Under clear skies, the pioneers climbed up the foothills of the Sierras and stopped to rest at a lake. That night, 5 feet of snow fell, blocking their passage on the summit. They retreated to the lake and prepared a winter camp: three cabins and three tents for more than 80 people. They tried to cross the mountains two more times, but they were forced to return to the camp.

Above: the route of the Donner Party across the Salt Lake Desert. These photos show some of the harsh terrain traveled by pioneers as they headed west.

In mid-December, after one man had died of malnutrition, 17 of the pioneers set out on snowshoes to seek help. At times, they faced 20-foot-high snowdrifts, but they reached the summit in two days—only to find that the snow was even deeper on the other side. Meanwhile, snow covered the cabins at the lake camp. To stay alive, people ate a kind of gruel made from boiled cowhides. By mid-February, many more would die, including Jacob.

James Reed and his wife, Margaret

Finally, one month after leaving the lake camp, seven snowshoers made it to a settlement. Relief parties were sent out to rescue the pioneers trapped on the other side of the mountains. Rescuers did not reach the lake camp until March, and it took almost two months for them to bring all of the survivors to safety.

TRUTH OR MYTH?

For years it was believed that members of the Donner Party ate each other to survive. New research shows that although this may be true, most likely it was among other members of the group and not the Donner family.

Almost a year after leaving Springfield, the final pioneer arrived at Sutter's Fort in California. Only 48 members of the party had survived.

THE CAMP TODAY

At Donner Memorial State Park in Truckee, California, where the Donner Party spent the winter of 1846, you can swim in Donner Lake, hike, and camp. Also, you can visit a historic site in the area that memorializes the Donner Party pioneers. A large boulder that formed the fireplace and part of the back wall of a makeshift cabin still can be seen, along with a plaque that includes the names of all of the Donner Party members.

THE FIRST GREAT GOLD RUSH

(No—it was not in California.)

One day in 1828, a young man named Benjamin Parks went deer hunting near the tiny town of Licklog, Georgia. The rolling hills were home to the Cherokee nation, a Native American tribe, and wilderness settlers. As Benjamin was walking along, he stubbed his toe on a rock that was the color of egg yolk. It was gold!

Benjamin told some friends about his find, and then they told some more people, and within a few years, about 15,000 fortune seekers had moved to the area. The early settlers would hardly have recognized their little communities—or known what to call them. Instead of trees, miners' camps and cabins, or shanties, sprouted all over the hills. Licklog was renamed Dahlonega, a Cherokee word that means precious metal, gold, and yellow money. Nearby Nuckollsville became Auraria, from the Latin word for gold.

During the day, the springs and creeks were full of prospectors panning for gold nuggets, while large, steam-powered dredges scraped

the riverbeds and digging equipment cut tunnels into the mountains. Big strikes, or finds, were common. At night, everyone celebrated their good luck, singing and dancing around campfires.

Instead of using money, miners paid for things with gold dust and nuggets. Most people carried their entire fortunes in small pouches in their pockets. Some miners hid their pouches in hollow trees and shallow holes in the ground—but this proved to be a bad idea, as the stashes were sometimes lost or stolen.

Instead of using money, miners paid for things with gold dust and nuggets.

By 1836, Dahlonega was an important community, and its citizens built a courthouse in the center of town—some say right over a vein of gold. The brick used to build it contained flecks of gold that sparkled in the sunlight. So much gold was being mined in the area that the next year, the U.S. government built a mint in Dahlonega. From 1838 to 1861, it produced more than $6 million worth of coins.

The southern gold rush ended when the California gold rush began, in 1849. Soon after that, the outbreak of the Civil War forced the mint to close. Mining continued, but not on the same scale.

The town of Dahlonega as it looked in the early 1900s.

CONTINUED

NOT EVERYBODY GOT RICH

The prosperity that drew an influx of people to Georgia during the 1830s spelled doom for the state's Cherokee nation. Miners overran tribal lands, causing hardship and hard feelings, and some local authorities did little to discourage this behavior. By 1838, most members of the Cherokee tribe were forcibly escorted to land west of the Mississippi River. Some hid and were taken in by white families. The march west, in which thousands of Cherokees died from starvation and exposure, is known as the infamous Trail of Tears.

SITTING ON A FORTUNE

In February 2006, workers renovating the dining room of the Smith House restaurant and hotel in Dahlonega, Georgia, discovered a 19-foot-deep shaft under the floor. One man who went into the shaft discovered footholds carved into the side of it (for climbing) and evidence of tunnels off of it. Historians claim that in 1884, Captain Frank Hall, who owned the land, requested a permit from town officials to dig for gold there. When they refused to grant him one, he built the house to cover his mining operation.

Did You Know?

The Georgia State Capitol dome is covered with 60 ounces of gold from Dahlonega mines.

The COLOR of MONEY

The U.S. government began printing paper money in 1862 to pay for the Civil War. Union soldiers called the bills "greenbacks" because of the distinct green color on the back. When the Bureau of Engraving and Printing changed the design in 1929, they continued using green ink. The green ink was available in large quantity, the color was resistant to wear, and people identified the color green with prosperity.

Confederate soldiers were paid with money that was blue or gray. Can you guess what they called it? (Answer at bottom.)

Be a DOLLAR SCHOLAR

- **The U.S. government prints nearly $700 million worth of money every day, almost half of it as $1 bills.**
- **The portrait of a living person can never appear on any U.S. currency.**
- **Only one woman has appeared on U.S. paper currency: Martha Washington.**
- **There are no images of African-Americans on U.S. paper currency, but three appear on U.S. coins: peanut farmer and agriculturist George Washington Carver, teacher and writer Booker T. Washington, and baseball player Jackie Robinson.**
- **U.S. paper currency is not paper—it is 25 percent linen and 75 percent cotton.**
- **A loon appears on the back of a Canadian dollar coin. As a result, the Canadian dollar is often called a "loonie."**

Answer: Bluebacks and graybacks.

Three Little

The President's Bear

President Theodore Roosevelt, whose nickname was Teddy, was a great outdoorsman. In 1902, he went to Mississippi on business. While there, he embarked on a hunting trip. Several days passed without any bear sightings. On the last day of the hunt, one of the men in the hunting party caught a bear and tied it to a tree. Here was a bear for the president to shoot! The man thought that the president would be pleased, but Teddy said that he wouldn't kill a bear that couldn't defend itself.

Soon Clifford Berryman, a cartoonist, heard about the bear and drew a picture of it tied up, with Teddy Roosevelt turned away. The cartoon was published in *The Washington Post* and thousands of people saw it. One of these was Morris Michtom, a poor shopkeeper in Brooklyn, New York. Morris was so touched by the president's decision that he asked his wife, Rose, to make a toy bear to celebrate the occasion. Rose

BEAR FACTS

- **Today, almost any stuffed toy bear is called a "teddy bear."**
- **One of the original Teddy bears is in the Smithsonian National Museum of American History.**

Bears

sewed pieces of plush brown fabric into a bear form, stuffed it, and added buttons for eyes. Morris put the little bear on display in his shop window, with a sign that read, "Teddy's Bear." To his surprise, many people offered to buy it. Instead, Morris sent the toy bear to the White House as a gift for the president, with a letter asking for permission to use the name Teddy for additional toy bears that he hoped to make and sell. The president granted his request.

"Teddy bears" became so popular—and generated so many orders—that Morris and Rose started a toy factory to keep up with the demand.

The Children's Bear

A. A. Milne and his son Christopher Robin.

In 1914, during World War I, Lt. Harry Colebourn was traveling from Winnipeg, Manitoba, to eastern Canada. From there he would then be transported to Europe to join the 2nd Canadian Infantry Brigade. At a train stop in White River, Ontario, Harry, who was a veterinarian, bought a female black bear cub for $20 from a hunter who had killed her mother. Harry named the bear "Winnipeg" after his hometown. Her nickname was "Winnie."

Winnie went to England with the brigade and became its mascot. In December 1914, when Harry learned that the brigade was to be sent to France, he brought Winnie to the London Zoo to stay for a while.

CONTINUED

When the war ended, Harry realized that the zoo had become Winnie's home. On December 1, 1919, Harry formally donated Winnie to the zoo, where she lived until she died in 1934.

During her time at the London Zoo, Winnie became popular with visitors, including the son of author A. A. Milne, Christopher Robin. Christopher and other children sometimes played with Winnie in the cage, even going for short rides on her back!

Christopher had a teddy bear named Edward Bear, but he later changed its name to Winnie-the-Pooh, after his favorite animal at the London Zoo.

A. A. Milne published his book *Winnie-the-Pooh* in 1926. The book described the adventures of a special group of woodland inhabitants, based on Christopher's stuffed animals, including the teddy bear renamed Winnie-the-Pooh for the well-loved real bear from Canada.

BEAR  **FACTS**

- **The name Pooh was originally the name of a swan that lived near the Milne home.**
- **Today, a bronze statue of Winnie stands at the London Zoo.**

The Smokey Bear

In 1942, during World War II, a Japanese submarine staged an attack that started a fire at an oil field close to the Los Padres National Forest near Santa Barbara, California. The event made government officials concerned that enemy attacks could start other forest fires. To help prevent that from happening, the U.S. Forest Service and other officials issued posters about fire safety and national security. One poster used Bambi to show people how much harm fires can cause.

Eventually, the officials decided to use a bear to symbolize all of the wildlife in the forest. They named the symbol Smokey Bear, after

"Smokey" Joe Martin, a firefighter who had been the assistant chief of the New York City Fire Department from 1919 to 1930. On August 9, 1944, an illustrator named Albert Stachle created the first Smokey Bear poster, showing the bear wearing a forest ranger's hat and blue jeans and pouring water onto a campfire.

Smokey Bear's popularity spread like wildfire.

Then, in 1950, a fire raced through the Lincoln National Forest in the Capitan Mountains of New Mexico. While putting out the fast-spreading flames, firefighters discovered a bear cub that had climbed a tree to escape the fire. The bear was flown to Santa Fe to get treatment for burns on its legs and paws. He recovered and was later presented by the New Mexico state game warden to the chief of the Forest Service, to serve as a living symbol for the campaign for fire prevention and conservation. Named "Smokey," the fortunate bear found a home at the National Zoo in Washington, D.C., where he lived for his remaining 26 years.

BEAR FACTS

- **Smokey Bear once received so much mail that he was given his own zip code.**
- **In 1984, Smokey became the first individual animal to be honored on a postage stamp.**

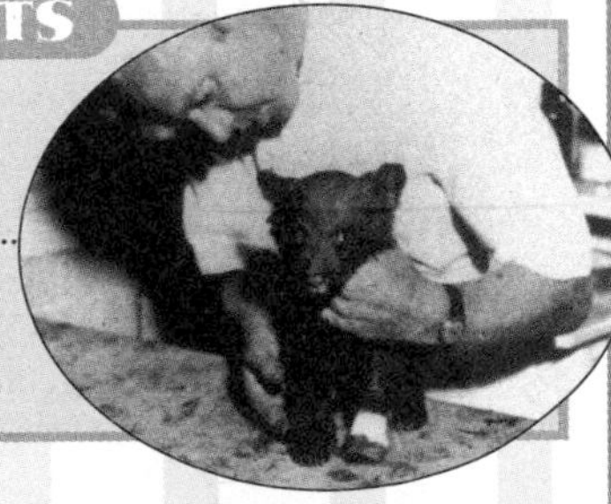

The SCOOP on ICE

THROUGH

A.D. 56–68

Roman emperor Nero is believed to have sent slaves into the mountains to fetch snow to mix with fruit and honey.

618–907

Chinese rulers have "ice men" lug ice to the palace, where it is used to make a fermented milk treat.

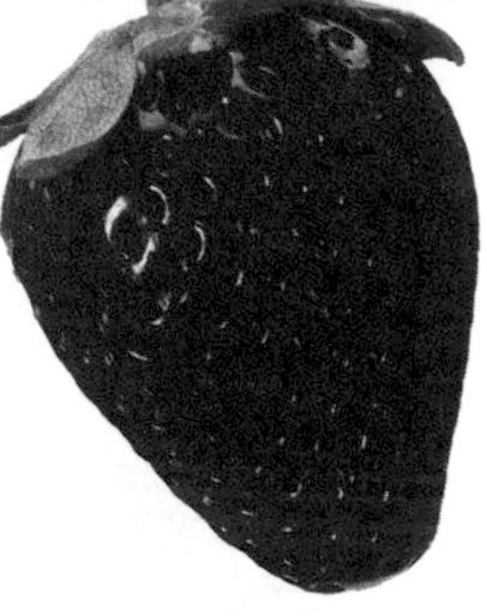

1744

For the first time on record, American colonists dine on strawberries and ice cream. It happens in Annapolis, Maryland.

1782–1817

American presidents Washington, Jefferson, and Madison treat guests to ice cream at inaugurals and special dinners.

SPRINKLES

In 1988, the world's biggest ice cream sundae was made in Edmonton, Alberta. It weighed more than 24 tons.

CREAM
THE AGES

1840
A serving of ice cream purchased on a steamboat costs six cents.

1860
Most towns have an ice cream parlor or saloon. Vanilla is the most popular flavor.

1866
Street vendors pushing carts and wheelbarrows sell ice cream and ice milk called "hokeypokey" in cities.

1870s
Ice cream makers offer many flavors, including chocolate, tutti-frutti, rice, cinnamon—even asparagus!

1878
The first mechanical ice cream scoop is patented.

1880s
The ice cream sundae, probably named for the day of the week and costing five cents, becomes popular.

CONTINUED

SPRINKLES The top five favorite flavors of

ICE CREAM

1890

A concoction made with sweetened milk, carbonated water, and a raw egg, called a milk shake, becomes popular with men.

1899

Hokeypokey vendors in New York City start selling ice cream sandwiches for two or three cents.

1893

Fried ice cream, also called Alaska pie or fritter, is introduced at the Chicago World's Fair.

1904

Ernest A. Hamwi makes and serves the first ice cream cone, at the St. Louis World's Fair.

1893

A magazine declares the ice cream soda—a mixture of shaved ice, sweet cream, flavored syrup, and soda water—to be America's "national beverage."

1918

During World War I, eating ice cream is considered patriotic because the United States has a surplus of dairy products.

the United States are vanilla, chocolate, Neapolitan, strawberry, and cookies 'n' cream.

1920
Harry B. Burt of Youngstown, Ohio, makes the first ice cream on a stick.

It takes 50 licks, on average, to eat a single-scoop cone.

1920
Christian Nelson in Onawa, Iowa, invents the chocolate-dipped Temptation I-Scream Bar. His advertising slogan becomes, "I scream, you scream, we all scream for the I-Scream Bar."

1921
The I-Scream Bar is renamed the Eskimo Pie. In 1927, it becomes the first ice cream bar to be sold in nickel vending machines.

1925
The first Howard Johnson ice cream stand opens, in Wollaston, Massachusetts.

1930
I. C. Parker of Fort Worth, Texas, invents a chocolate-nut sundae on a sugar cone and calls it a Drumstick.

CONTINUED

1934

Former radio salesman Thomas Carvel opens his first ice cream store, in Hartsdale, New York.

1935

Ice cream is shipped by plane from Salt Lake City, Utah, to Warm Springs, Georgia, for a Thanksgiving dinner hosted by President Franklin D. Roosevelt.

1938

J. F. McCullough and his son, Alex, serve the first soft ice cream, in Kankakee, Illinois. Shortly thereafter, they open the first Dairy Queen, in Joliet, Illinois.

1940s

Burton Baskin opens an ice cream parlor, and his brother-in-law, Irvine Robbins, opens an ice cream store. They soon combine forces to become one company, Baskin-Robbins.

1943

Military doctors prescribe ice cream to soldiers recovering from combat fatigue.

1973

Boston taxi driver and ice cream stand owner Steve Herrell originates "mix-ins"—a choice of candy bits and cookies added to a scoop.

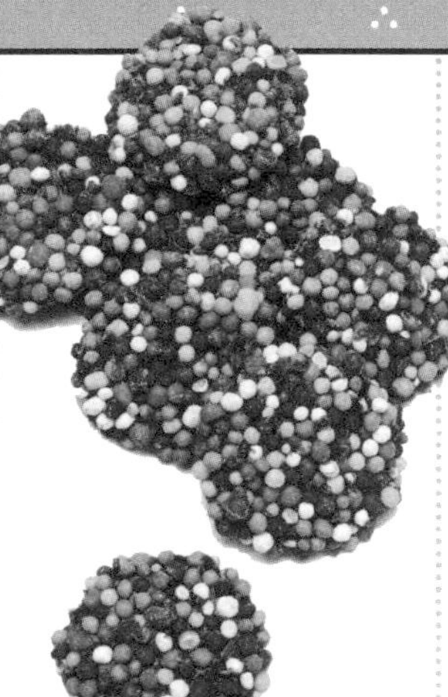

2006

Dreyer's Grand Ice Cream opens one of the world's largest ice cream plants, in Laurel, Maryland.

1978

Having passed a $5 correspondence course in ice cream making the year before, Ben Cohen and Jerry Greenfield open their first Ben & Jerry's ice cream shop in Burlington, Vermont.

1985

A St. Louis, Missouri, custard stand owner blends soft serve and fruit juice to make "concrete." This treat soon becomes the Dairy Queen Blizzard.

BE A (SODA) JERK

Find easy-to-make ice cream and soda fountain recipes at **Almanac4kids.com/guide.**

***CAUTION:**
Never feed your pets chocolate, as it may be toxic to them.

RIGHT ON, LEFT-HANDERS!

Years ago, some teachers insisted that all students, including left-handers, learn to write with their right hand. Teachers thought that students would have an easier time if they were not "different" from right-handed writers. Some thought that using the left hand was just a bad habit. Some even slapped or punished left-handed kids who had trouble. Now we know that everyone should use whichever hand is most comfortable.

Today, 10 to 12 percent of the world's population is left-handed. It's not surprising that lefties sometimes feel "left out." Plenty of superstitions and odd terms exist:

- Many people believe that the devil is LEFT-HANDED.
- The Latin word for LEFT, *sinister,* also means unlucky, evil, and suspicious.
- The French word for LEFT, *gauche,* also means clumsy.
- A LEFT-HANDED compliment is an insult.
- A LEFTIST favors changing the established government or order, usually to benefit the common man.

Facts and Folklore

A LEFT-HANDED baseball pitcher is called a southpaw. (There is no such thing as a northpaw.)

Scientists aren't sure what causes lefthandedness. Genetics plays a part, but it's not the whole story. For example, identical twins have the same DNA, but it is common for one twin to be right-handed and the other to be left-handed. Many left-handers have a symmetrical brain, meaning that the left and right portions of their brain are shaped alike. Right-handers often have an asymmetrical brain: The left cerebral hemisphere is often larger than the right cerebral hemisphere.

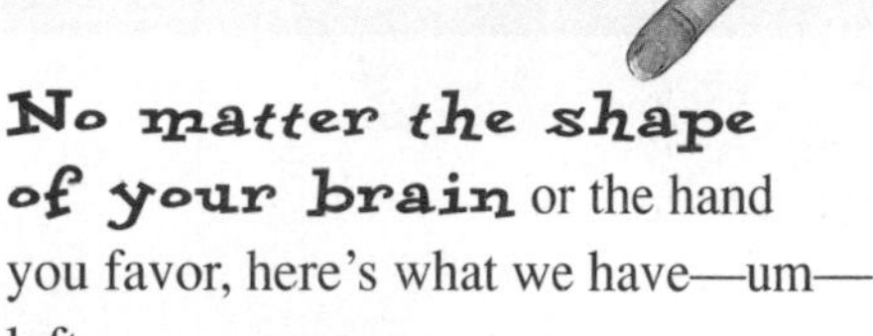

No matter the shape of your brain or the hand you favor, here's what we have—um—left . . .

THE LEFT TEST. There's no surefire way to measure "handedness." One of the most widely used tests is called the Edinburgh Handedness Inventory, developed in Edinburgh, Scotland, in the 1970s. This test asks participants which hand they most often use for a series of activities, including writing, eating, drawing, throwing, cutting with scissors, brushing teeth, and unscrewing a lid.

Left-handed Burgers? Baloney!

A full-page ad in *USA Today* in 1998 claimed that Burger King had developed the "LEFT-HANDED WHOPPER." The burger had the same fixings, but they were turned 180 degrees so that they wouldn't drip out on left-handed customers. It was a joke! The ad ran on April 1 (April Fools' Day).

Lefties Day. **August 13 is INTERNATIONAL LEFT-HANDERS DAY. The tradition was started in 1992 by the Left-Handers Club, a group in the United Kingdom. Club members around the world give interviews and play left-handed games.**

Left-hander Heaven? **Lefties might want to travel to LEFT HAND, WEST VIRGINIA, where there is a church, a school, and a post office. The village was so named because it sits on the left-hand fork of the Big Sandy River, not because of the way its citizens write.**

Left-handed Reward. A few left-handers attending Juniata College in Pennsylvania have benefited from a SCHOLARSHIP JUST FOR LEFT-HANDERS established in 1979 by Mary and Frederick Beckley, two left-handers who met when they attended a tennis class together in 1919.

Try Your Hand

If you're right-handed, try writing with your left. If you're left-handed, try brushing your teeth with your right. You're likely to find these activities surprisingly difficult.

Mind MANGLERS

PUNNIES

1. What flowers can be found between the nose and chin?
2. What do you get if you cross a sheepdog with a rose?
3. Which state needs a tissue?

NIFTY NUMBERS

1. When do 2 and 2 make more than 4?
2. How much dirt is there in a hole 5 feet deep, 6 feet long, and 3 feet wide?
3. Why isn't your nose 12 inches long?

SILLY SENSE

1. Which is heavier, a half Moon or a full Moon?
2. Why is a dog dressed more warmly in summer than he is in winter?
3. What did one hurricane say to the other hurricane?
4. Why did the lion spit out the clown?
5. What happens when it rains cats and dogs?

LETTER LOGIC

1. What is the longest word in the English language?
2. Change these words into one word: One hug
3. If you take away two consecutive letters from this five-letter word beginning with "d," only one will remain. What is the word?
4. This title for a lady is written the same both forward and backward. What is the word?

Turn to page 187 for the answers

ASTROLOGY for Pets

When was your pet born? See if its personality match

CAPRICORN

December 22–January 19

Capricorn pets are easy to train. They follow commands, work hard, and like to be active.

ARIES

March 21–April 20

Aries pets are energetic explorers. You can count on them to be active, curious, and a bit demanding.

AQUARIUS

January 20–February 19

Aquarius pets are smart but unpredictable. They like to roam and do not always do as they are told.

TAURUS

April 21–May 20

Taurus pets are stubborn but dependable. They return affection, appreciate good food, and don't like change.

PISCES

February 20–March 20

Pisces pets are gentle and appreciate patient owners. They need their own "spot" (pillow, bed, perch, or rug).

GEMINI

May 21–June 20

Gemini pets are smart, fun, and very playful. They are curious about everything and love toys.

he characteristics of its sign.

CANCER

June 21–July 22

Cancer pets are faithful guardians. All they want in return for their loyalty is affection and good food.

LIBRA

September 23–October 22

Libra pets like company—either other animals or people. They aim to please and are most unhappy when left alone.

LEO

July 23–August 22

Leo pets are leaders. They have lots of energy and are always ready to play, but they are also strong protectors of their homes.

SCORPIO

October 23–November 22

Scorpio pets are smart but stubborn. Always into things, they have curiosity that often leads to mischief.

VIRGO

August 23–September 22

Virgo pets are smart, easy to train, and quick to housebreak. They especially like to be groomed.

SAGITTARIUS

November 23–December 21

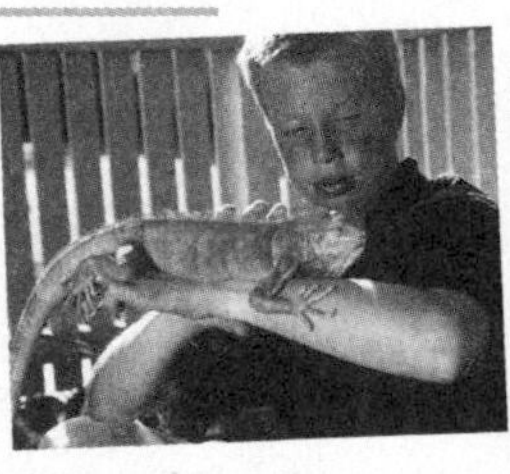

Sagittarius pets are energetic adventurers. They like to get out—and not just in the backyard.

HOCUS-PO

NOBODY KNOWS EXACTLY who played the first magic trick, but it was probably an ancient Egyptian. An Egyptian scroll dating from 1700 B.C. was found depicting Dedi of Dedsnefu performing the cups-and-ball illusion for a pharaoh. (You've probably seen this trick: The magician places three cups upside down on the table. He then puts a ball underneath one of the cups. But when he picks up a different cup, the ball seems to have jumped invisibly from underneath the original cup to underneath the new one.)

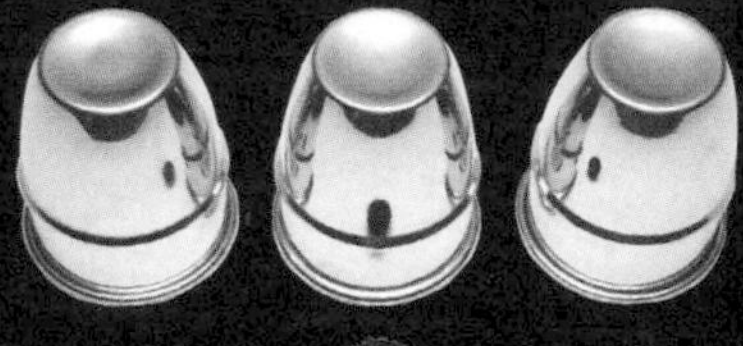

ANCIENT GREEKS AND ROMANS also practiced magic, but they made it a sort of religion. They staged "miraculous" events, such as rigging the doors of temples to open spontaneously and fixing statues so that wine or water flowed from their mouths on cue. Even kings believed that these magicians had supernatural powers and asked them to change the weather, get rid of enemies, cure diseases, and cast out evil spirits.

IN THE MIDDLE AGES (A.D. 500–1450), people thought that magic was witchcraft and magicians were evil. Some were jailed and some were executed. Not until the Renaissance (1450–1600) did it become permissible for magicians to travel in shows and perform for the public.

CUS!

continued

DURING THE 1700S, magicians began to be accepted as entertainers, doing tricks, reading minds, making objects disappear, and more. One, Wolfgang von Kempelen, was famous in his day for devising a "magically" automated chess player. In 1783, Benjamin Franklin played against the machine and lost.

FINALLY, BY THE 19TH CENTURY, performing magic had become a popular pastime. During this period, French watchmaker and performer Jean Eugène Robert-Houdin began performing realistic illusions, even seeking help from scientific experts to make the tricks convincing. Robert-Houdin, who became known as the father of modern magic, served as an inspiration to many magicians. One of these was Ehrich Weiss, who called himself Harry Houdini, in tribute to the watchmaker.

HOUDINI'S DEATH-DEFYING MYSTERY

FAILURE MEANS A DROWNING DEATH

BECOME A MAGIC MAKER
The Society of American Magicians (SAM) was founded on May 10, 1902, in New York City. Through SAM, magicians meet and learn tricks. Its Society of Young Magicians (SYM) is for kids ages 7 to 17. To learn more, go to **Almanac4kids.com/puzzles.**

MAGIC MEDICINE?

During the Middle Ages, people thought that the word "ABRACADABRA" could cure illness. They wrote the word 11 times in an upside-down triangle shape on a piece of paper, eliminating one letter in each line. Then they wore the paper around their neck and spoke each line. They thought that this would make their disease fade away.

abracadabra
abracadabr
abracadab
abracada
abracad
abraca
abrac
abra
abr
ab
a

The FOUR KINGS Trick

THE PREPARATION: **Without letting your audience see you, find and remove the four kings from a deck of playing cards. Pile them face up in your palm. Take three other cards and stack them face up, directly under the kings.**

THE TRICK: **Fan out the kings face up for your audience to see, making sure that only the four kings are visible and that the back of the fan is not. Now tell this story:**

"There once were four kings staying in a hotel. Their room was on the top floor."

- **Collapse the fan and put the seven cards face down on top of the deck.**

"The kings were hungry, so they called for room service. The first king said that he wanted to take a swim before the food arrived, so he went to the pool."

- **Take the top card from the deck and carefully put it on the bottom of the deck without letting anyone see it. (This will not be a king, but your audience will think it is.)**

"The second king wanted to buy a souvenir, so he went down to the gift shop."

- **Take the top card in the deck and put it on the bottom of the deck.**

"The third king decided to get some exercise before eating, so he went to the hotel's gym."

- **Once again, take the top card and put it on the bottom of the deck.**

"When room service arrived, the fourth king called them all back up to the room."

- **Knock three times on the deck. Wave your hand and say a few magic words, such as:**

"Abracadabra! Ring-a-ding-ding! The next four cards will be a king!"

- **Now, one by one, flip over the top four cards to reveal the kings–and take a bow!**

JUMPING FOR JOY

People have been jumping, or skipping, rope for centuries. In ancient Egypt, skipping rope was considered a boy's sport. Early ropes were made from grapevines, and it is believed that jumping rope might have been part of an ancient ritual to help crops grow—the higher the jump, the taller the plants would be.

Early Dutch settlers brought the activity to the American colonies in the 1600s, but even then it was considered to be mostly a boy's pastime. People believed that skipping rope could be harmful for girls. One book from the mid-1800s claimed that if girls jumped rope too much, their blood vessels could burst, and, it asked, "What could possibly be more unladylike than collapsing in a bloody heap right there on the front lawn!"

By the late 1800s, however, newspapers began to advertise jump ropes for sale to all children. Such advertisements claimed that by jumping rope a child could "find graceful movement, healthful exercise, and amusement."

By the early 1900s, skipping rope had become a popular activity for girls. Prizefighters, too, began jumping rope to get in shape for their boxing matches because it strengthened their leg muscles, increased their lung capacity, and helped them to be quick on their feet.

Today, people of all ages jump rope to stay in shape. Proponents claim that just 10 minutes of skipping rope provides the same health benefits as running for 45 minutes, and that jumping rope . . .

- improves balance and agility
- improves coordination and flexibility
- increases muscle strength
- strengthens the heart

Most of all, it's **FUN!**

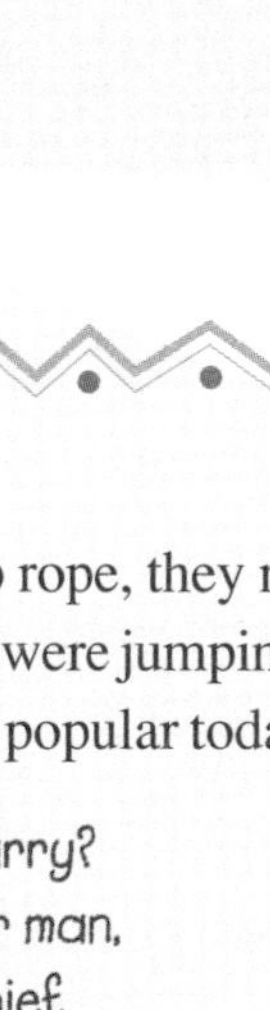

SWING TIME

Once girls began to jump rope, they made up rhymes that they chanted while they were jumping. This favorite from the early 1900s is still popular today:

> Whom will I marry?
> Rich man, poor man,
> Beggarman, thief.
> Doctor, lawyer,
> Merchant, chief.

A "Teddy bear" rhyme was common while Teddy Roosevelt was president (see "Three Little Bears," page 120). In addition to jumping while two others twirled the rope, the jumper also had to perform the physical tasks mentioned in the rhyme without tripping.

Teddy bear, teddy bear,
Turn around.
Teddy bear, teddy bear,
Touch the ground.
Teddy bear, teddy bear,
Shine your shoe.
Teddy bear, teddy bear,
That will do.

In this rhyme, several people have to jump together at the same time. (Before you start, decide who will jump in and when.)

I had a little puppy.
His name was Tiny Tim.
I put him in the bathtub to see if he
could swim.
He drank up all the water, he ate a
bar of soap.
The next thing you know, he had a
bubble in his throat.
In came the doctor. (person jumps in)
In came the nurse. (person jumps in)
In came the lady with the alligator
purse. (person jumps in)
Out went the doctor. (person jumps out)
Out went the nurse. (person jumps out)
Out went the lady with the alligator
purse. (person jumps out)

FANCY FOOTWORK

Once you can jump rope with ease, try these variations:

DOUBLE UNDERS

Keep your feet together and jump, making two turns of the rope for every one jump.

TRIPLE UNDERS

Same as above, but make three turns of the rope for every one jump.

DOUBLE DUTCH

This is a rope jumping technique for advanced jumpers. Two players each hold the ends of two ropes and spin the ropes in opposite directions, like the blades of an eggbeater. A third person jumps in and has to jump over both ropes without tripping.

DID YOU KNOW?

- Two New York City policemen made double Dutch jump roping a WORLD-CLASS SPORT by organizing the first Double Dutch Jump Rope Tournament, held on February 14, 1972.
- Bloomer, Wisconsin, calls itself the Jump Rope Capital of the World. Every year since 1960, the town has held a CHAMPIONSHIP JUMP ROPE CONTEST for elementary school–age children. Contestants speed jump, and the person who is able to jump over the rope the most times during a given period (usually 10 seconds) is the winner.
- Hundreds of jump rope associations in the United States and Canada sponsor COMPETITIONS for all ages. Test your skill! Find out more at Almanac4kids.com/outdoors.

Longest Distance Skipped

In 1963, 71-year-old Tom Morris skipped a rope 1,264 miles from Brisbane to Cairns in Australia.

Fastest Skipper

In 1982, Albert Rayner skipped a rope 128 times in 10 seconds in Birmingham, England.

Most People to Jump on One Rope (for at Least 12 Turns of the Rope)

In 1992, 260 students from Yorkton Regional High School in Yorkton, Saskatchewan, jumped over a 100-yard-long rope in unison.

The Ropeless Jumper

In 2006, inventor Lester J. Clancy of Mansfield, Ohio, was issued a U.S. patent for a cordless jump rope. To simulate the rope action, users swing handles attached to doughnut-shape rings that are weighted with small balls. Jumping is optional.

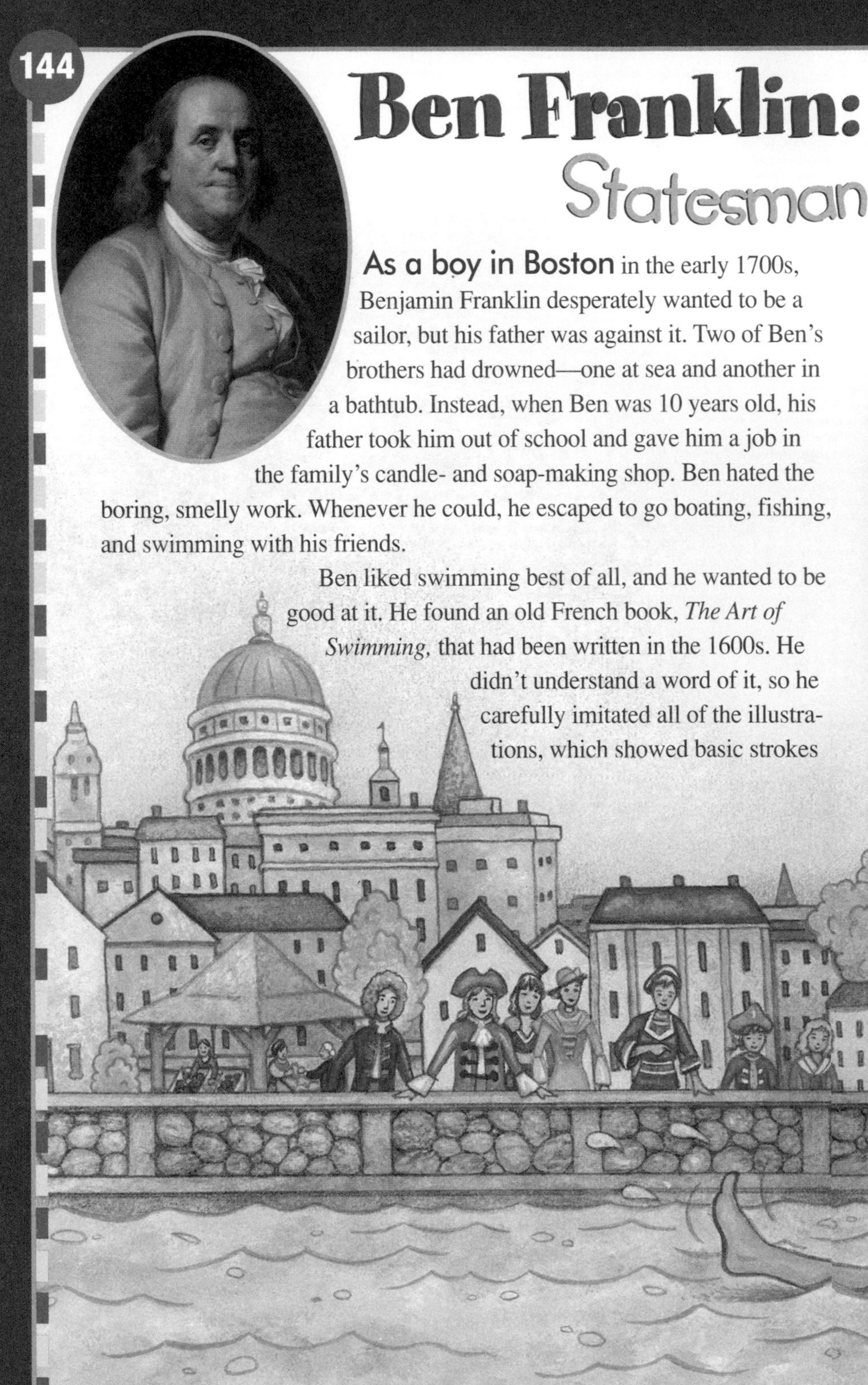

Ben Franklin: Statesman

As a boy in Boston in the early 1700s, Benjamin Franklin desperately wanted to be a sailor, but his father was against it. Two of Ben's brothers had drowned—one at sea and another in a bathtub. Instead, when Ben was 10 years old, his father took him out of school and gave him a job in the family's candle- and soap-making shop. Ben hated the boring, smelly work. Whenever he could, he escaped to go boating, fishing, and swimming with his friends.

Ben liked swimming best of all, and he wanted to be good at it. He found an old French book, *The Art of Swimming,* that had been written in the 1600s. He didn't understand a word of it, so he carefully imitated all of the illustrations, which showed basic strokes

Scientist . . . Swimmer?

as well as such tricks as diving, swimming with one foot, and clipping your toenails underwater. Soon he had learned all of the strokes in the book.

Ben began inventing new ways to swim faster and more easily. When he was 11, he made a pair of swim fins from wood for his hands. The fins made his wrists tired, but with them he could swim farther. He also designed flipperlike sandals, but they didn't work as well.

As a teenager, Ben continued to enjoy showing off his swimming skills. One day, while living in London and boating on the Thames River with friends, he took off his clothes, jumped into the water, and swam away. He swam three and a half miles downriver and, along the way, performed tricks on and under the water for onlookers who had gathered on the riverbanks. As word of his skills spread, people suggested that he give swimming lessons. A friend offered to pay him to start a swimming school, and an Englishman wanted him to teach his sons how to swim. Ben turned down the offers because he missed his sweetheart Deborah Read, who was in Philadelphia.

continued

Ben never lost his love for swimming and the sea. He recommended swimming courses for the school he established in 1751 in Philadelphia. He wrote about lifesaving techniques and how to rescue people from shipwrecks with lifeboats.

Ben's aquatic skills also came in handy during the American Revolution. At age 70, he outwitted English spies who were on his trail in Paris by swimming to a barge in the Seine River, where he conducted secret meetings. Years later, he taught his grandson Benny how to swim by swimming across the Seine every morning.

In 1968 (almost 200 years after his death), Ben was inducted into the International Swimming Hall of Fame in Fort Lauderdale, Florida. Today, a bust of him stands in the boardroom. Ben would have appreciated the honor. He always liked making a big splash.

COOL, DUDE!

Nine-year-old Benjamin Franklin may have invented kiteboarding—sort of. One afternoon, while flying a paper kite with a friend beside a pond, Ben had a brainstorm: He undressed and asked his friend to carry his clothes to the far side of the pond, about a mile away. Then, still holding onto the kite, Ben stepped into the water, floated on his back, and let the kite pull him along. He learned that by raising and lowering the kite he could change his speed. Towed by his kite the entire way, he traveled effortlessly to where his friend was waiting.

The GAME Game

Match each term with its sport or activity. Answers below.

	Term		Sport or activity
_____	**1. Balk**	**A.**	**Baseball**
_____	**2. Bonk**	**B.**	**Basketball**
_____	**3. Carom**	**C.**	**Bowling**
_____	**4. Catch a crab**	**D.**	**Football**
_____	**5. Dink**	**E.**	**Ice hockey**
_____	**6. Grind**	**F.**	**Rowing**
_____	**7. Lollipop**	**G.**	**Skateboarding**
_____	**8. Red zone**	**H.**	**Skiing**
_____	**9. Schuss**	**I.**	**Snowboarding**
_____	**10. Slash**	**J.**	**Soccer**
_____	**11. Tip-off**	**K.**	**Surfing**
_____	**12. Touch out**	**L.**	**Swimming**
_____	**13. Trap**	**M.**	**Tennis**
_____	**14. Turkey**	**N.**	**Track & Field**
		O.	**Volleyball**

Answers

1. A (an illegal movement by a pitcher); 2. I (to bounce off an object such as a rock, tree, or stump); 3. E (a rebound of the puck off the boards or any other object); 4. F (to stroke an oar and miss the water or dig too deeply); 5. M (a soft return that causes the ball to drop after crossing the net); 6. G (to slide along the edge or top of an object); 7. O (a gentle serve; make too many lollipops and you get licked); 8. D. (the imaginary area between the defense's 20-yard and goal lines); 9. H (to ski downhill fast and straight, often in a full-tuck position); 10. K (a quick turn off the top of a wave); 11. B (the jump ball that starts a game); 12. L (to reach the touch pad first and win a race); 13. J (to use your chest, thighs, or feet to slow down and control a moving ball); 14. C (three strikes in a row). Not used: N. Track & Field.

GOT BAIT?

These fishing baits will catch most freshwater panfish. (A panfish is one that will fit whole into a skillet for cooking.) Use small worms and grasshoppers to catch bluegill, crappie, perch, porgy, and sunfish. Use large worms to catch carp, trout, bass, and catfish.

WORMS

Look for earthworms and night crawlers (large earthworms) . . .

- in the morning, after rain, on driveways and sidewalks and under rocks
- under old boards, bricks, logs, or debris where the soil is moist
- in compost or manure piles, under leaves, or in mulch and rich soil
- at night, using a flashlight with a red cover over the bulb. Earthworms don't have eyes, but their skin is sensitive to light. They respond to a flashlight beam, but they do not "see" red light.

CAN 'EM

Get a large coffee can with a plastic lid. Punch small holes in the lid. Loosely fill two-thirds of the can with soil. Stir in some moss mixed with sand or cornmeal. (The grit will "polish" the worms as they crawl around. Fish like shiny worms!) Feed the worms used coffee grounds and vegetable scraps, but only what they will eat in about two days. (Do some experimenting to find out what the proper amount is.) Ten to 12 worms should live for about a week.

HOOK 'EM

Hook the worm (or a large one cut in half) two or three times through the middle and leave a bit of the worm's head and tail to wiggle. Fish like lively worms!

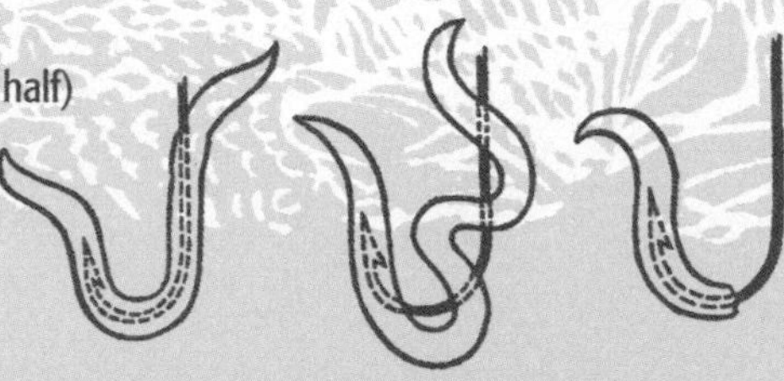

GRASSHOPPERS

Look for grasshoppers early in the morning in fields and gardens. Here are three ways to catch them:

- Move toward the grasshopper slowly and quietly. Cup it with both hands.
- With one hand, hold the mouth of a jar under the grasshopper. With your other hand, gently guide the grasshopper into the jar. Close the lid.
- With a friend, run through a field holding a bedsheet up between you.

CAN 'EM

Get a large coffee can with a plastic lid. Punch holes in the lid. Put a handful of grass into the can. Feed the grasshoppers moist vegetable scraps. Ten grasshoppers should live for a couple of weeks.

HOOK 'EM

Grasp the grasshopper firmly and push the hook through its body as shown below. Either method works well.

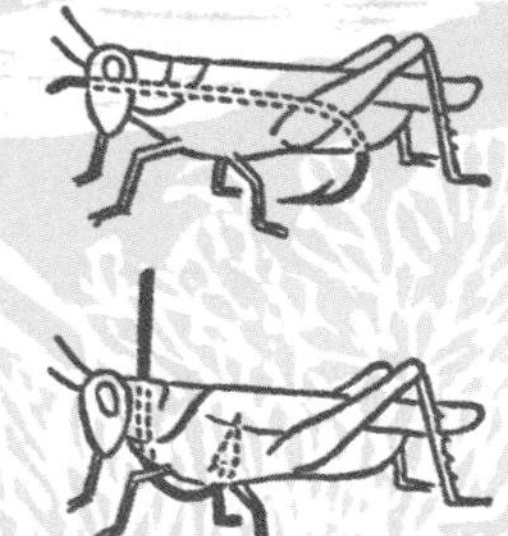

HOW TO CATCH A FISH

- When you feel a tug on your line and it gets pulled under the water, a fish has taken the bait and is swimming away. Give your rod a jerk to "set" the hook in the fish's mouth. Start reeling in!

Sunfish

Yellow perch

FISH TALES

Did your fish get away? Or did you catch a big one? Tell everybody about your fishing trip at **Almanac4kids.com/tellus.**

Catfish

Brown trout

HOOKS, LINES, AND SINKERS

1. What fish likes to gossip?
2. What fish likes to catch a tan?
3. What fish chases a mouse?
4. What fish can perform operations?
5. What fish is the most valuable?
6. What fish goes well with peanut butter?
7. Why are fish so smart?
8. What is the best way to communicate with a fish?

Bluegill

ANSWERS: 1. Largemouth bass 2. Sunfish 3. Catfish 4. Sturgeon 5. Goldfish 6. Jellyfish 7. Because they live in schools. 8. Drop it a line!

Crappie

Ready to Reel 'Em In?

Get a list of what you need when you go fishing, when to fish, and more at **Almanac4kids.com/outdoors.**

Smallmouth bass

Note: Fish images not to scale.

Baseball: GET A GRIP!

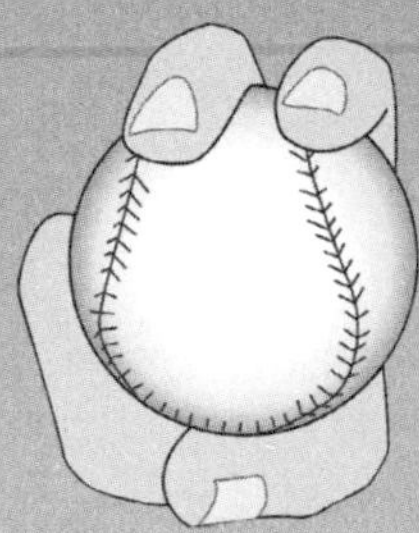

Curveball

A "bender" veers or breaks to the left when thrown with the right hand and to the right when thrown with the left hand.

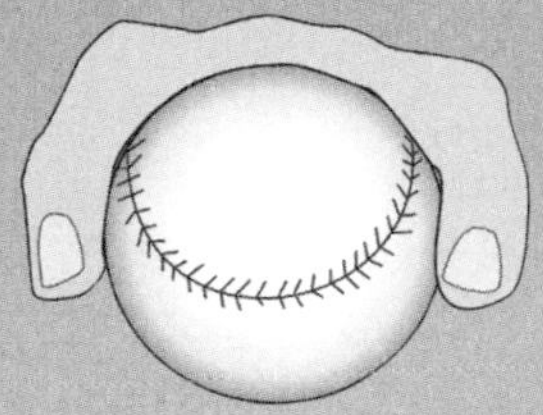

Forkball

A pitch with the ball placed between the index and middle fingers so that the ball takes a sharp dip near home plate.

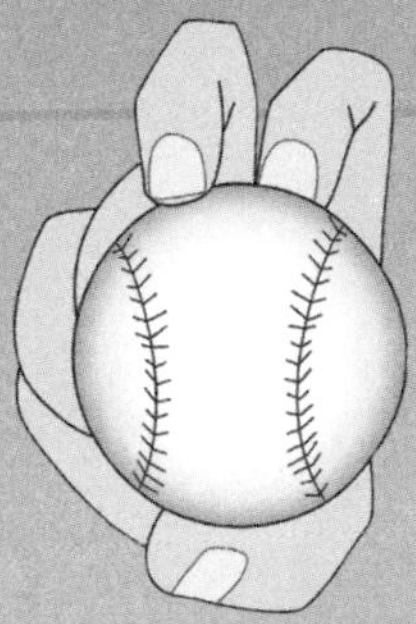

Knuckleball

A slow, randomly fluttering pitch thrown by gripping the ball with the tips or nails of two or three fingers.

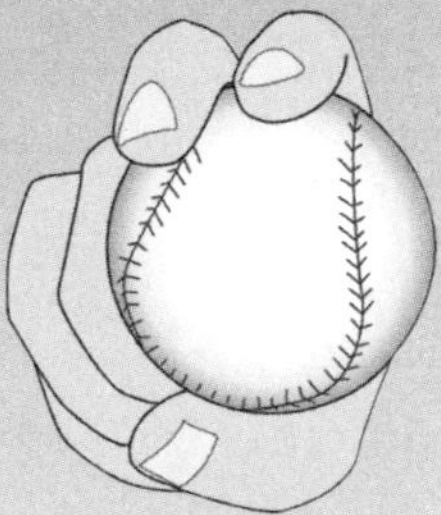

Slider

A fast pitch that breaks at the last moment in the same direction as a curveball.

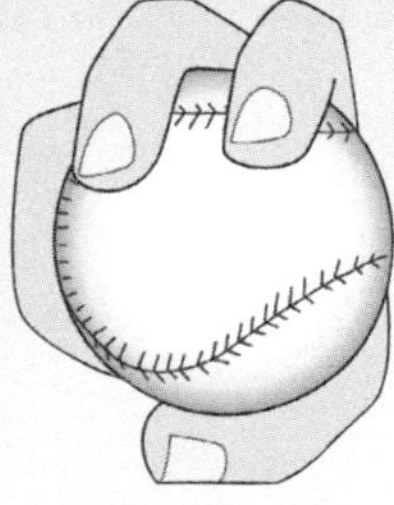

Fastball

A pitch thrown at the pitcher's maximum speed.

Note: Check with a parent or coach before throwing curveballs, forkballs, and sliders. They might hurt your arm.

Lou Gehrig Babe Ruth Jackie Mitchell

YOU GO, GIRL!

IN 1931, Joe Engel, owner of a Tennessee minor league baseball team called the Chattanooga Lookouts, wanted to create some excitement for his team and their fans. Joe had heard about a left-handed 17-year-old pitcher from Fall River, Massachusetts, whose lifelong ambition was to pitch to—and strike out—baseball legend Babe Ruth of the New York Yankees.

Joe scheduled an exhibition game between the Lookouts and the Yankees in Chattanooga. He signed the determined player from Fall River, a *girl* named Jackie Mitchell, to a contract.

Jackie got her chance on April 2, midway through the first inning. Fans in the packed stadium cheered as 36-year-old Babe, also known as the "Sultan of Swat," came up to bat. Stepping into the batter's box, he tipped his hat to Jackie, who was on the mound. She studied him, wound up, and threw her trademark fastball. It sunk low and was called ball one.

Babe stepped out of the batter's box and looked at Jackie. He shook his head, moved back in, and got ready for the next pitch. Jackie wound up, and the ball came blazing in over the plate. Babe swung—and missed. He then swung at Jackie's next pitch and missed that, too. Strike two.

All eyes were on Jackie as she set her sights, wound up, and delivered the next pitch. Babe never moved his bat as the umpire yelled, "Strike three—you're out!" The fans erupted with cheers as Babe walked back to the Yankees bench, shaking his head.

Next in the lineup was another Yankee legend, Lou Gehrig. He swung at Jackie's first three pitches, missed them all, and quietly walked back to the dugout to sit next to Babe.

A lengthy (estimated at ten minutes) standing ovation took place before Jackie faced the next batter, Tony Lazzeri. After Jackie walked him, Joe stood up in the Lookouts' dugout and motioned for her to come in off the mound. Jackie was done for the day.

Even though the Yankees eventually won the game, Jackie Mitchell remains forever in the annals of baseball.

POSTGAME ROUNDUP • **Some newspaper reporters and critics claimed that Babe and Lou had struck out on purpose, but both men said that they had truly tried to hit Jackie's fastballs. She became known as "The Girl Who Struck Out Babe Ruth."**

Ladies' FIRSTS

1898 Lizzie Arlington becomes the first woman to sign a minor league contract.

1974 Young girls are granted permission to play in Little League.

1992 American Women's Baseball Federation (AWBF) is founded to organize regional and national championships.

1997 The Women's Baseball League is formed to provide opportunities for women athletes to play baseball.

2001 The AWBF and the Women's Baseball Association of Japan sponsor the first Women's World Series.

2006 A life-size statue honoring the women athletes of the All-American Girls Professional Baseball League is installed at the National Baseball Hall of Fame in Cooperstown, New York.

Ride 'Em,

FOLLOW THE HERD

A young female bovine is a HEIFER.
A young male bovine is a BULL CALF.
An adult female bovine is a COW.
An adult male bovine is a BULL.

Rodeos are competitions held in a fenced, dirt-surfaced arena, either indoors or outdoors. At these events, cowboys and cowgirls show off their skills, such as bareback riding, steer wrestling, calf roping, and barrel racing. One of the most popular events is the bull-riding

Cowboy!

contest. Cowboys ride bulls that weigh as much as 2,000 pounds.

Rodeo bulls are specially bred to compete. They are fed a diet of high-protein feed and alfalfa hay, which gives them extra nutrients for more speed and power. Rodeo bulls often live well into their teens, which is considered old for bulls.

DID YOU KNOW?

A "bullfighter" jumps into the ring when a rider is thrown off a bull. He or she distracts the bull, giving the cowboy a chance to run out of the ring safely.

continued

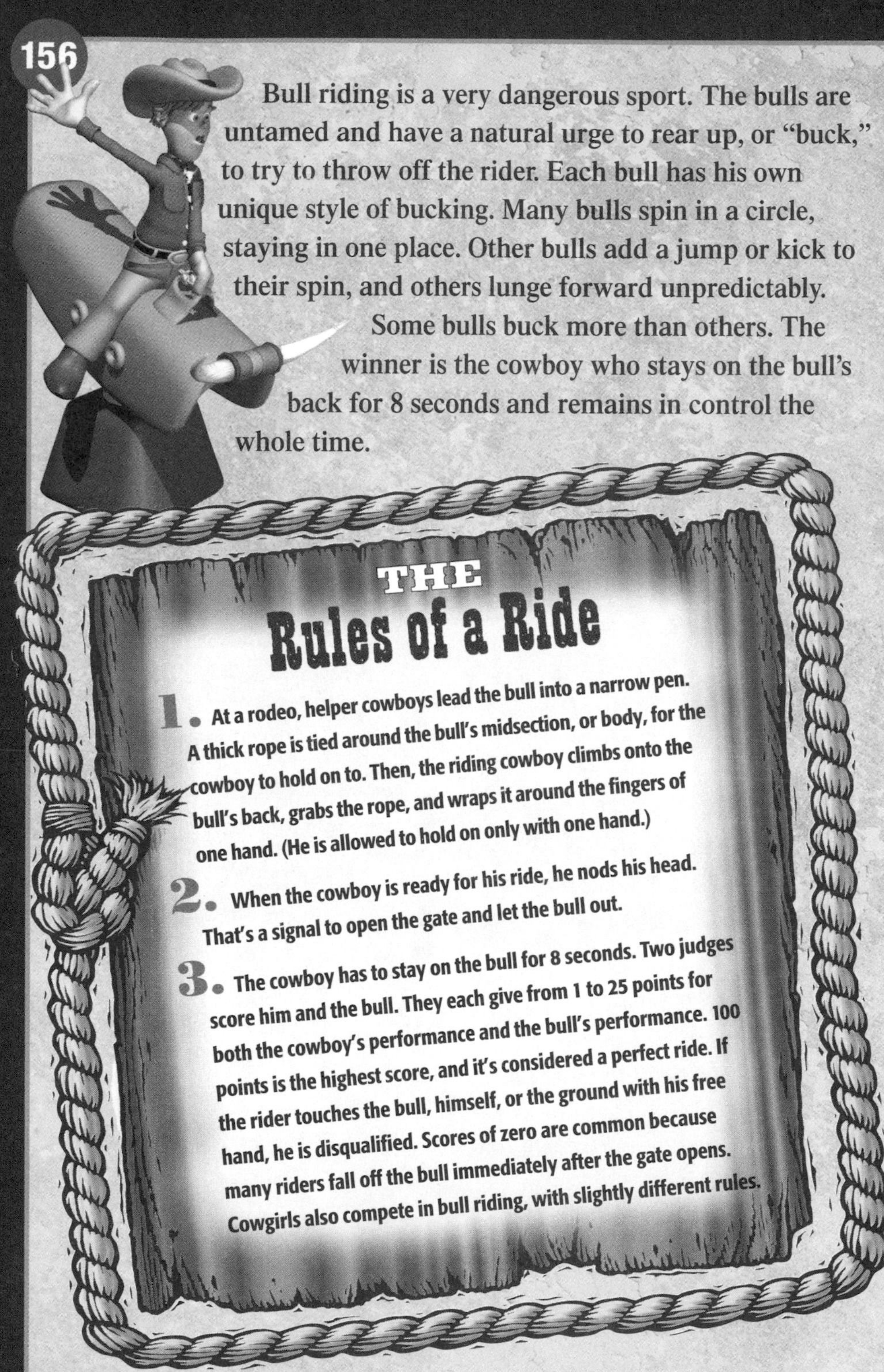

Bull riding is a very dangerous sport. The bulls are untamed and have a natural urge to rear up, or "buck," to try to throw off the rider. Each bull has his own unique style of bucking. Many bulls spin in a circle, staying in one place. Other bulls add a jump or kick to their spin, and others lunge forward unpredictably.

Some bulls buck more than others. The winner is the cowboy who stays on the bull's back for 8 seconds and remains in control the whole time.

THE Rules of a Ride

1. At a rodeo, helper cowboys lead the bull into a narrow pen. A thick rope is tied around the bull's midsection, or body, for the cowboy to hold on to. Then, the riding cowboy climbs onto the bull's back, grabs the rope, and wraps it around the fingers of one hand. (He is allowed to hold on only with one hand.)
2. When the cowboy is ready for his ride, he nods his head. That's a signal to open the gate and let the bull out.
3. The cowboy has to stay on the bull for 8 seconds. Two judges score him and the bull. They each give from 1 to 25 points for both the cowboy's performance and the bull's performance. 100 points is the highest score, and it's considered a perfect ride. If the rider touches the bull, himself, or the ground with his free hand, he is disqualified. Scores of zero are common because many riders fall off the bull immediately after the gate opens. Cowgirls also compete in bull riding, with slightly different rules.

★★ The Rodeo Star ★★

RED ROCK was one of the greatest rodeo bulls in history. He was born on a ranch near Sisters, Oregon, and was named after a rock formation near his owner's ranch. When Red Rock was two years old, he was sold to a man who bought bulls for rodeos. In 1983, Red Rock performed in his first rodeo. He was competitive *and* gentle. He threw off every cowboy who tried to ride him—309 in a row. But unlike most other bulls, he didn't chase the riders after they were thrown. His owner said, "He has all the character of a well-mannered person."

A cowboy named Lane Frost studied videotapes of Red Rock to figure out how to ride him. Lane was thrown off several times, but he didn't give up. In 1988, at the "Challenge of the Champions" in Redding, California, he became the first cowboy to ride Red Rock. The two eventually met up four more times, with Lane successful in three of them. In 1990, Lane Frost and Red Rock were inducted into the Pro Rodeo Hall of Fame in Colorado Springs, Colorado. The bull attended the ceremony and then served as an ambassador for the sport of rodeo for the rest of his life, which ended on June 8, 1994.

Two-Wheeling

Backpedaling
Have you ever heard that Leonardo da Vinci sketched an early design for a bicycle in the 1490s? Not true! The famous artist and inventor did once draw two wheels close together. Later, a jokester added pedals, a chain, and more bikelike details. Da Vinci did not invent—or even envision—the bicycle.

Scottish blacksmith Kirkpatrick Macmillan makes the first pedals and attaches them to the front wheel.

1817

German Karl von Drais unveils a two-wheel wooden machine with iron tires that he propels by pushing his feet against the ground. He names the contraption after himself: the Draisienne. Other people call it the "hobbyhorse," the "velocipede" (meaning "fast foot"), and the "running machine." It is banned on sidewalks.

1839

1861

Frenchman Pierre Michaux improves on the pedals, but because metal tires make for a very bumpy ride, people start calling these contraptions "boneshakers."

Through Time

About 85 million people in the United States ride bicycles—and millions more in other countries do, too. How did all of these wheels get rolling?

People start using the term "bicycle."

In England, small-and-big-wheel bikes are called "penny farthings" after two coins: a penny, which is small, and a farthing, which is large.

AROUND 1870

James Starley of Coventry, England, begins to manufacture bikes with a front wheel that is up to five feet in diameter and a much smaller rear wheel. The larger wheel size increases the distance traveled with each turn of the pedal. When the bikes tip over, riders often bump their heads—an event that becomes known as "taking a header."

CONTINUED

A U.S. bike builder creates the American Star, which has a big wheel in back and a small wheel in front.

Designers make bikes with all-metal frames and rubber tires, and place pedals so that they turn gears and a chain attached to the rear wheel.

Will Robertson rides an American Star down the steps of the U.S. Capitol very early in the morning, to avoid being arrested.

1880

1885

Ladies in long skirts find that big-wheel bikes can be dangerous, so they and other folks start riding adult tricycles, or three-wheelers.

Englishman John Kemp Starley (James's nephew) introduces the Rover Safety Bicycle. Its wheels are the same size, so the bike is easier to get on and off, balance, and stop. Safety bike factories spring up all over.

Amazing Annie

On June 25, 1894, Annie Cohen Londonderry, a young mother who had just learned how to ride a bike, declared to onlookers at the Massachusetts State House that she would circle the world

1888

Bike clubs form, and tracks, trails, and routes are mapped. Some rowdy riders, known as "scorchers," race their bikes through city streets at breakneck speeds and cause trouble.

Irish veterinarian John Dunlop discovers that air-filled inner tubes cushion a ride, so he puts them into the tires of his son's tricycle.

1889

There are about 200,000 Safety bikes in the United States. (Ten years later, there are more than a million.)

1894

Following the invention of the car and motorcycle, bikes become less popular with adults and more popular with kids.

A California bicycle shop owner starts using bikes for a delivery service between Fresno and San Francisco.

on her bike (not counting some ocean crossings, of course). She completed her amazing adventure in Chicago 15 months later.

CONTINUED

"Major" Racing

- **Major Taylor worked at a bike factory in Worcester, Massachusetts, in 1895. Three years later, he held seven world bike-racing records. In 1899, he won the one-mile world championship in Canada, becoming the second African-American world-champion athlete (the first was a boxer named George Dixon). Time after time, however, Major was banned from races or encountered prejudice because of his skin color.**

It's a Bird, It's a Plane, It's a . . . Bike?

- **What has pedals and looks like a hang glider with an enclosed cabin area? The *Gossamer Albatross*—a flying bicycle. On June 12, 1979, Californian Bryan Allen flew it over the English Channel, from England to France. The 23-mile flight took 2 hours and 49 minutes.**

The *Gossamer Albatross II*, a backup for the original *Albatross*, was flown as part of NASA's low-speed flight research.

1919

Companies start making kids' bikes with fenders, headlights, and even fake gas tanks like motorcycles. Some weigh 65 pounds!

1930

Tullio Campagnaro, a former amateur bike racer, receives a patent for the quick-release hub.

1978

Schwinn introduces the "Airdyne" stationary bike.

Glacier Glider

- In March 1998, a French racer named Christian Taillefer set the record for fastest biking down a glacier, with a speed of 132 mph in Vars, France.

Go, Wheels, Go!

- The record for the greatest distance ever biked in 12 hours is 280.9 miles, set on August 31, 2002, by 35-year-old Marko Baloh in the Novo Mesto Velodrome, an outdoor bicycle track in Slovenia.

Fantastique!

- On July 24, 2005, American Lance Armstrong *(right)* won the Tour de France, the world's most grueling race, for a record-breaking seventh consecutive year.

Side by Sideways

- In 2006, Boston inventor Michael Killian *(right)* developed a sideways bike with handlebars on the front and back. The rider sits and pedals forward, but can steer the bike to drift to the side, like skis.

2007

- Bicycles are used for everything from circling in driveways to pedaling along bike paths to making deliveries and police patrolling—and through the years, the basic principles of bike design have stayed the same.

In With the GOOD AIR, Out With the BAD

What really happens when you take a deep breath? The air you breathe into your nose and mouth when you inhale travels down your throat (called the **pharynx**), past the voice box (called the **larynx,** which contains your vocal cords), and on to the windpipe (called the **trachea**). From there, it branches into your left or right main **bronchial tubes** and then into your two lungs. In your lungs, the bronchial passageways branch more and more and get smaller and smaller until they become tiny **bronchioles.** At the ends of the bronchioles are **alveoli,** which are tiny air sacs shaped like bunches of grapes.

'S not just funny, it's CILI . . . A!

Lining the bronchial passageways are tiny hairs called cilia. These hairs are constantly waving, moving mucus—a thick, sticky liquid. Another place you have mucus is in your nose, where it is also called snot or boogers. Glands in your nose produce more than a pint of mucus each day to catch unwanted particles and germs that you breathe in and to keep air passages moist. The cilia in your nose move the mucus back toward the throat, where it is swallowed. If you have a cold or allergies, too much mucus may collect and you'll end up with a runny nose. When this happens, grab a tissue and blow!

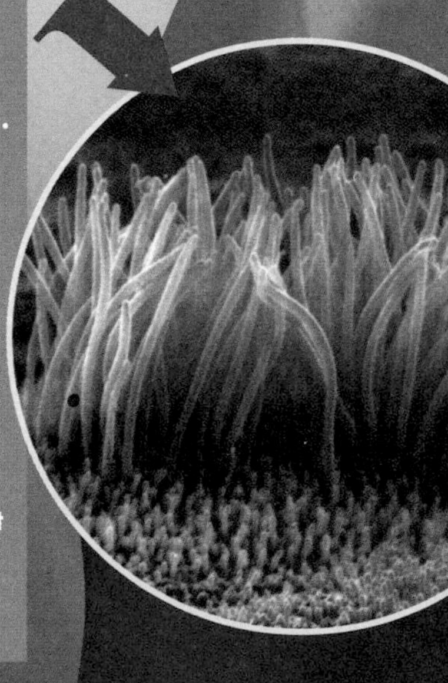

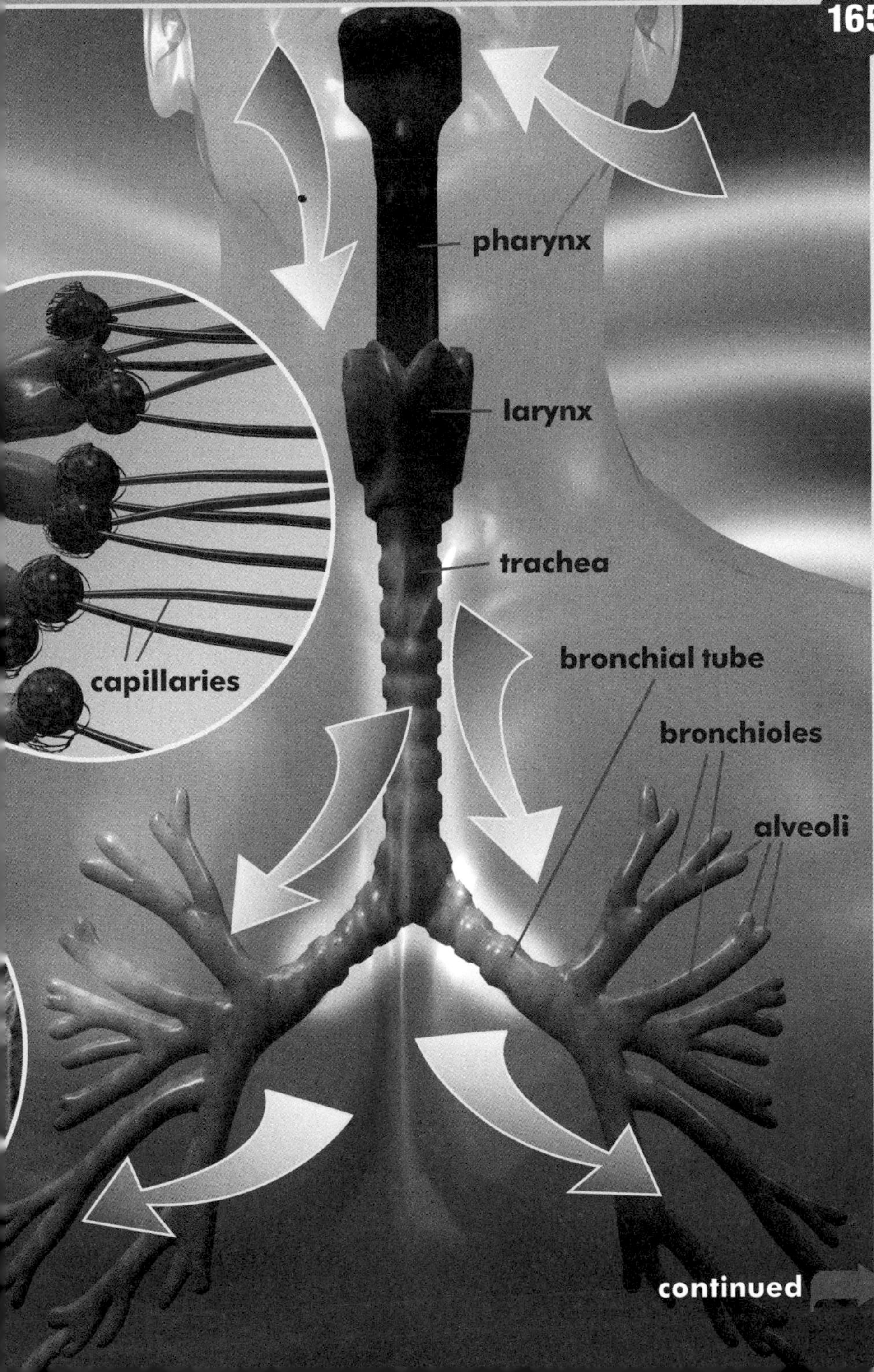

pharynx

larynx

trachea

capillaries

bronchial tube

bronchioles

alveoli

continued

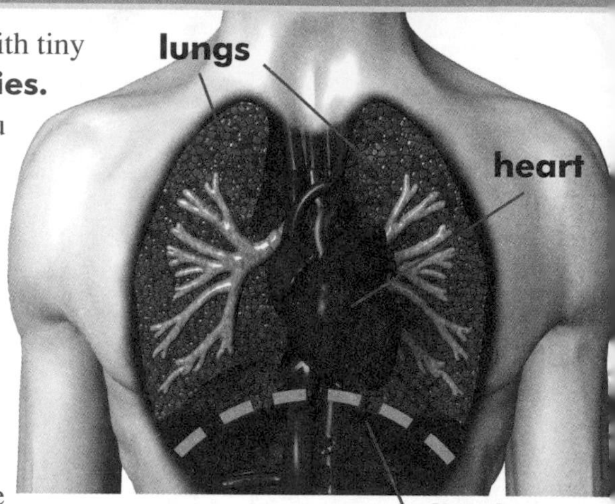

The alveoli are in touch with tiny blood vessels called **capillaries.** Good air—the oxygen that you **inhale**—passes through the alveoli, through the walls of the capillaries, and into your bloodstream. Your blood carries the **oxygen** to other parts of the body. At the same time, your blood releases bad air—**carbon dioxide**—into the alveoli. The carbon dioxide is transported out of your body in the opposite way that the oxygen came in. Any oxygen in your air passageways that didn't reach the alveoli when you inhaled, and all other gases in the air that your body can't use, are also **exhaled.**

The big wall of muscle in your chest that makes this all possible is called the **diaphragm.** When you inhale, the diaphragm moves down, creating suction to pull air into your nose and mouth and on through the bronchial passageways, causing your lungs to expand. When you exhale, the diaphragm moves up, squeezing the air out of your lungs and forcing it to move on out through your nose and mouth. The muscles between your ribs also help you to breathe, by lifting your ribs up and out when you inhale and pulling them back when you exhale.

Did you know?

Your left lung is a little smaller than your right. This is so that there is enough room for your heart.

The term "SMOG," meaning a fog full of smoke and pollutants, came from combining the words "smoke" and "fog."

Did you know?

Kids breathe in 50 percent more air per pound of body weight than adults do.

What is this stuff called AIR?

Earth's air contains about 78 percent nitrogen and 21 percent oxygen. Other gases, such as argon, carbon dioxide, ozone, neon, helium, krypton, and water vapor, are present in tiny amounts. **Air can also contain . . .**

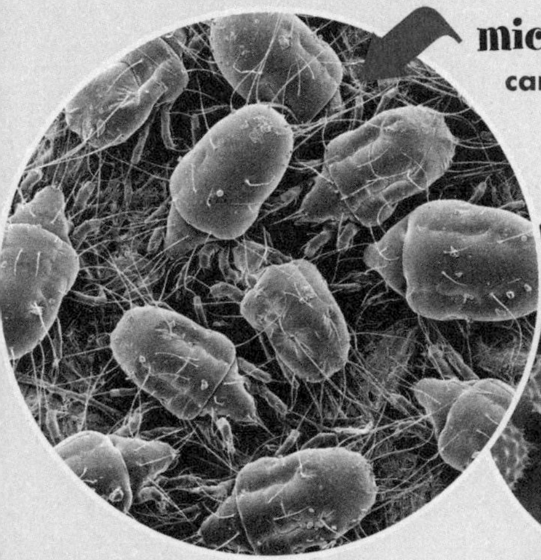

microbes, creatures so small that we can't see them. These include dust mites, bacteria, and viruses.

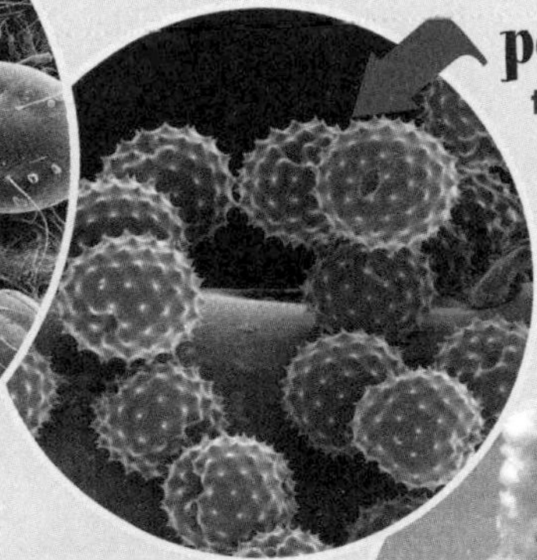

pollen, tiny grains produced by flowers to help plants form seeds

dirt, dust, and debris kicked up by wind or produced by fires and active volcanoes

pollutants, gases or particles (such as carbon monoxide, lead, nitrogen oxides, and sulfur dioxide) released into the air from industrial processes, vehicles burning fuel, and other sources

Most people, plants, animals, and microorganisms need the oxygen in air or water to turn food into energy. When energy is created, carbon dioxide is formed as a waste product, along with water.

Nearly all plants use carbon dioxide and water to help make food from sunlight in a process called **photosynthesis.** When food (in this case, a type of sugar called glucose) is made, oxygen is formed as a waste product and released into the air. If there weren't any plants, there wouldn't be enough oxygen for life on Earth!

For Crying Out Loud

An onion can make people CRY, but there has never been a vegetable invented to make them LAUGH.

–Will Rogers, American humorist (1879–1935)

Ever wonder why you cry when you are sad, or even when you're happy? Can you explain why your mom or dad cries when cutting up an onion? Do you know that you have tears in your eyes right now?

Your eyes have glands that make **three kinds of tears: basal, reflex,** and **emotional.**

Eyes need to be lubricated, and basal tears keep them wet. Your eyes make basal tears constantly—5 to 10 ounces of them every day. (That's anywhere from ½ cup to a little more than 1 cup of tears!)

These tears are made up of fatty oils (called lipids), water with a little bit of salt, and mucus. Every time you blink, your eyelids spread **basal tears** over the surface of your eyeballs. Tear ducts in the corners of your eyes serve as drains, carrying these tears into your nasal cavity.

Onion tears, or any tears caused by irritants such as fumes, wind, dust, or sand, are called **reflex tears.** You cry reflex tears automatically, whenever one or both of your eyeballs is irritated. Reflex tears power-wash the irritant away. These tears contain much more water than basal tears and are low in lipids and mucus.

Sad and happy tears are **emotional tears.** When you become upset or experience great joy, your brain sends a signal through your nervous system that causes your body to produce more proteins and hormones than it does when you are calm. When you shed emotional tears, you help your body to get rid of these extra chemicals, which helps to balance your body's stress level. That's why you sometimes feel better after you have a "good" cry.

Did You Know?

Babies don't cry tears until they are two months old.

Don't CRY because it's OVER. SMILE because it HAPPENED.

–Theodor Geisel, also known as Dr. Seuss, American writer (1904–91)

Z Z Z Z Z Z Z Z

You Are Getting Sleepy, VER-R-R-Y SLEEPY. . .

People today sleep less than people did hundreds of years ago. Why? Blame it on the lightbulb. As soon as Thomas Edison's invention came into homes, it became much easier for people to roam around at night.

> Early to bed,
> and early to rise,
> makes a man healthy,
> wealthy, and wise.
>
> *–Benjamin Franklin, American statesman (1706–90)*

We sleep because we need to rest. The brain needs time to recharge (sort of like a battery), and muscles, bones, and skin need time to grow and, if necessary, to heal. We fall asleep because at night the brain produces melatonin, a chemical that makes us sleepy.

Through the night, we sleep in repeating patterns, called cycles. Each lasts about 90 minutes and is divided into two categories:

- REM (rapid eye movement), or dream, sleep, when our eyes move back and forth quickly
- Non-REM sleep, which consists of light sleep, true sleep, deep sleep, and deeper sleep

Nobody really knows why we dream. Some researchers say that dreams help us make sense of what happened during the day. Other researchers believe that dreams represent things that are important, such as family, school, friends, and what you'll be when you grow up. Still others think that dreams are random—just electrical energy in the brain.

PILLOW TALK

Most of us spend about one-third of our lives sleeping: 8 hours per night, or 122 full days' worth per year!

Sleep—or lack of it—can affect your weight. Lack of sleep can stimulate chemicals in the body that make you feel hungry. Getting enough sleep reduces the chemicals—and your appetite.

Blind people dream—but if they have been blind since birth or very early in their childhood, they do not "see" things in their dreams. Instead, they dream of tasting, smelling, and touching things.

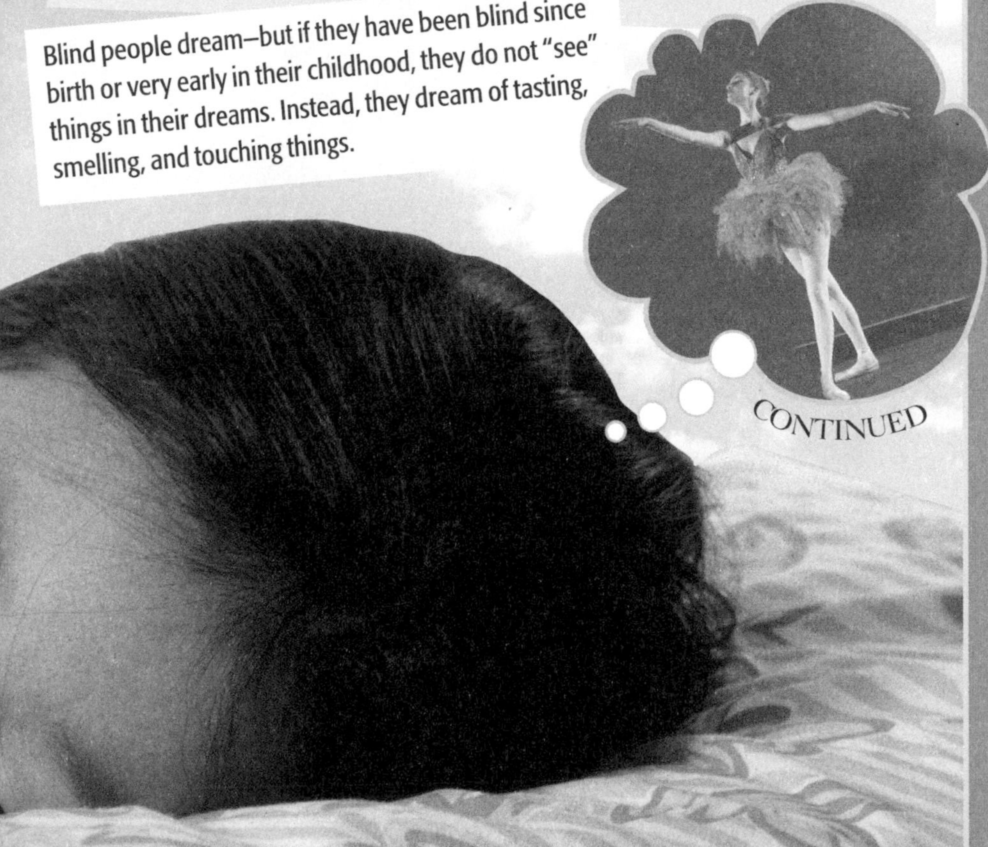

CONTINUED

SLEEP TIGHT!

ZZZ

Good night, sleep tight,
Don't let the bedbugs bite.

What's the scoop behind these lines from this old bedtime verse?

In colonial days, instead of mattress springs, beds had crisscrossed ropes, and the mattress went on top. Sometimes these ropes needed to be tightened so that the mattress wouldn't sag. "Sleep tight" means sleep comfortably.

BEDBUGS are tiny bugs that feed on human blood and often infested bedding in the old days.

PROJECT STAY AWAKE!

▸ **I**n 1965, high school senior Randy Gardner of San Diego, California, had an idea for a science fair project: to stay awake. The world's record—260 hours—had been set by a disc jockey in Hawaii, and Randy wanted to beat it.

He got help from a team of two friends and a sleep researcher. Randy didn't have much trouble until the third night, but from then on, he had to be watched every second so that he wouldn't doze off. He had the hardest time between 3:00 and 7:00 A.M. To keep him awake, the team talked to him, shook him, played the radio, took him for rides in a convertible, and played basketball with him. (This worked the best.)

Randy broke the record by staying awake for 263 hours—almost 11 days. When he finally went to bed, he slept for 14 hours and 40 minutes.

Don't try this at home! Lack of sleep can be dangerous.

ZZZZZZZZZZ DREAM DISCOVERIES

Writer Mary Shelley "dreamed up" the idea for Frankenstein in 1816. She was telling ghost stories one night and later, while she slept, the story came to mind. She started writing the next day and published her book two years later.

One morning in 1965, Beatles band member Paul McCartney woke up with a new tune in his head. Later, he added the words, and the song became "Yesterday." Today, this tune holds the Guinness World Record for the most recorded song.

While writer Robert Louis Stevenson was working on his novel *Kidnapped,* he had a weird dream. The ideas in it became the basis for *The Strange Case of Dr. Jekyll and Mr. Hyde,* published in 1886.

Want to remember your dreams? Keep a notepad by your bed and jot down what you remember when you wake up. Who knows what you might dream up?!

174 Know Why George Wash

George Washington wasn't an unhappy man (although he does look that way on the dollar bill!). The general, statesman, farmer, and Father of Our Country had bad teeth. His dental problems started when he was 24 years old and had to have a tooth pulled. For the next 30 years, he had many more teeth pulled because they were decayed and infected and his gums were swollen. (At that time, dentists used special hammers, saws, and chisels to do extractions.) Over the years, as his teeth were removed, his dentists made false teeth, or dentures, to fill the spaces. But these never fit very well.

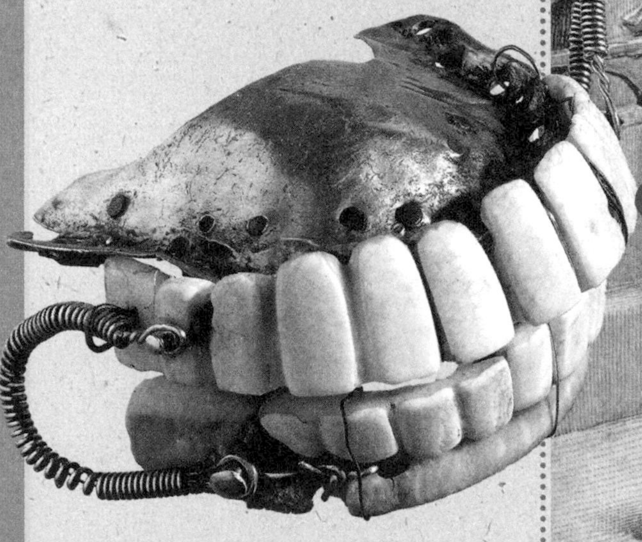

Then, George found a dentist named Dr. John Greenwood, who provided him with dentures that were made from

hippopotamus teeth and held together with metal springs. (The teeth weren't straight out of the hippo's mouth. Dr. Greenwood filed and sanded and polished them so that they looked like human teeth.) Unfortunately, the hippopotamus teeth didn't fit George's mouth very well either. They made talking and eating difficult, and they made his mouth pucker. He always looked like he was ready to give a kiss!

By 1789, when he became president, George had only one real tooth left in his mouth; all the rest were false. Right before his inauguration, George asked Dr. Greenwood to make him a set of dentures that would be comfortable and wouldn't cause him any embarrassment. The dentist got eight "new" teeth (supposedly, these came from dead people) to replace eight of the hippopotamus teeth. Even this was not a perfect fit. When George took the oath of office, his teeth slipped around in his mouth and made clicking noises.

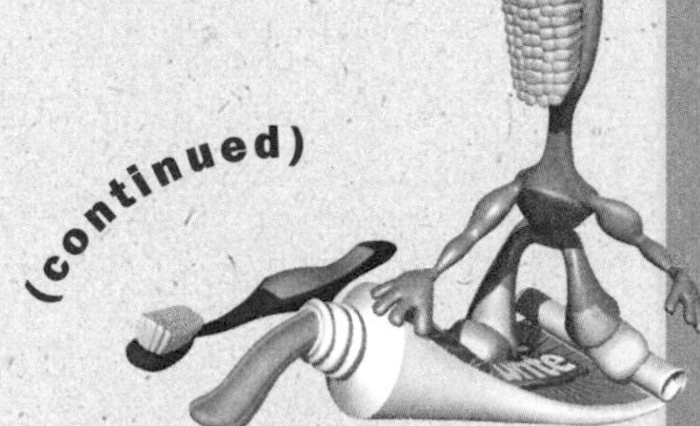

George put up with the bad fit and annoying clicks for about ten years. One day, he removed the false teeth from his mouth and mailed them back to Dr. Greenwood. He included a list of complaints about the teeth, including the fact that they pushed out his upper lip unnaturally. He didn't mention that the teeth had turned black—but the dentist noticed. He returned the dentures, fixed, with some advice in a letter. "Clean [the] false teeth after every meal," the dentist wrote, "and brush them with chalk dust!"

Brush Up on the Past

- Cavemen and -women used sticks, thorns, and quills to pick their teeth clean.
- Ancient Egyptians used a cream made of powdered oxen hooves and burned eggshells. (Some had slaves to pick their teeth for them.)
- In ancient China, soldiers' breath was so bad that a law was enacted to enforce tooth cleaning.
- Ancient Romans cleaned their teeth with bones, eggshells, oyster shells, and honey.
- The first bristle brushes to clean teeth were made in China in the 15th century, using hair from horses' manes or hogs.
- The first nylon-bristle toothbrush was introduced in 1938 by DuPont Laboratories. Now, that's something to smile about!

Bits to CHEW ON

- Just like fingerprints, everyone has a different set of teeth—even identical twins!

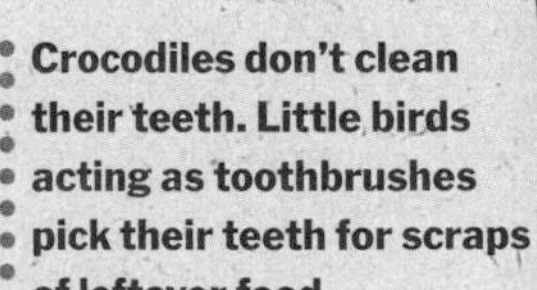

- The sperm whale has the largest teeth of any animal in the world. Its teeth are up to seven inches long and weigh up to two pounds.
- In 1996, a Belgian man pulled eight train cars weighing 493,563 pounds for 10 feet—by his teeth.
- Crocodiles don't clean their teeth. Little birds acting as toothbrushes pick their teeth for scraps of leftover food.

Warts Away!

Many people believe that you can get warts by touching a toad. They are so wrong! Warts—little flesh-color bumps on your skin—are caused by human papillomavirus. This virus can be transmitted from person to person, but more commonly it will spread from one area of your body to another. Children are more likely than adults to get warts, because adults usually have a greater immunity to them.

MOST WARTS disappear by themselves. Or, you can buy medications to get rid of warts at most drugstores. Years ago, if you wanted to get rid of a wart, you might have tried one of these 16 WACKY WAYS:

Simple and Easy

- ★ Count your warts each night for nine nights in a row.
- ★ Rub your wart with an onion.
- ★ Wash the area with the wart in water used to boil potatoes.
- ★ Rub a piece of chalk on the wart and then throw the chalk away.

Weird and Complicated

- ★ Rub it with coffee grounds, then put the grounds in a bag and bury them.
- ★ Without telling anyone, pick up a stone at midnight, spit on it, then put it on a rafter in the attic. After eight weeks, turn it over.

Slightly Gross

- ★ Tie a dog's hair tightly around the wart.
- ★ Rub it with a fish or a chicken's foot.
- ★ Kiss the wart, then kiss someone else.
- ★ Lick the wart first thing in the morning, before you eat or drink anything.

Very Gross

- ★ Rub it with cow's urine.
- ★ Mash ants on it.
- ★ Rub it with a snail or a rooster's head.
- ★ Cover it with cow manure.

Don't You Dare!

- ★ Prick the wart with a pin, put the blood on a cloth, and drop it in the path of a stranger. If he picks it up, he gets the wart.
- ★ Wish your warts on someone whose name you know, but whom you've never met.

Mayonnaise Magic

Did you know that the mayonnaise you put on your sandwiches and in potato salad can be used around the house? IT'S TRUE!

- Always use a spoon or other clean utensil—not your fingers!—when getting mayonnaise out of the jar for these projects.
- Store the mayonnaise in the refrigerator after opening.
- Tell your mom or dad before you try these tips.

Don't let **ROAD TAR** on your bike or skateboard slow you down. Spread a dab of mayo over the tar. Wait a few minutes, then wipe with a clean rag.

Oops! CRAYON MARKS on wooden furniture? Mayo will make them disappear. Using a clean rag or finger, rub a dab of mayo on the spot. Wait a minute or two, then wipe with a damp cloth.

Suffer no more from SUNBURN! A bit of mayo smoothed over the affected area will help relieve the pain and moisturize your skin.

To remove a TIGHT RING on your finger, cover the finger with mayonnaise and then gently pull the ring off.

STRENGTHEN YOUR NAILS with a mayo manicure! Put a few spoonfuls of mayonnaise into a small bowl. Plunge your fingernails into it and keep them there for five minutes. Wash with warm water.

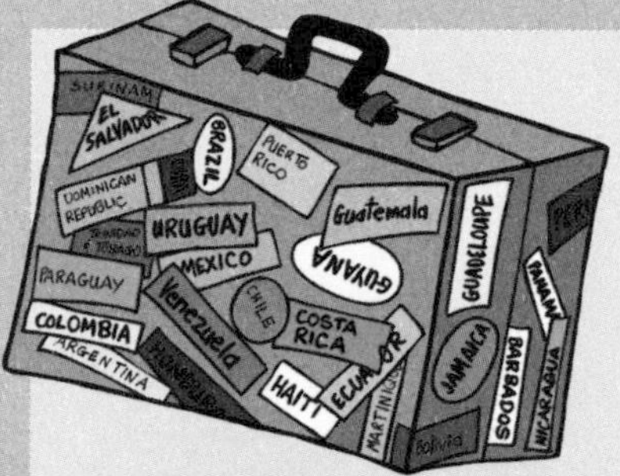

When STUBBORN STICKERS won't come unstuck, try this trick: Scrape off as much of the sticker as you can. Then cover any remaining residue with a thick coating of mayonnaise. Wait a few minutes. Use a clean cloth to wipe off the mayonnaise and residue.

Oh, no! **HEAD LICE!** Before going to bed, wash your hair and towel dry. Then apply mayonnaise all over your hair and scalp. (It must be real mayonnaise, not light or fat-free or salad dressing.) Cover your head with a shower cap and keep it on overnight. The next morning, rinse your hair with warm water and comb with a lice comb. Repeat this process for several days.

Got **GUM IN YOUR HAIR?** Rub mayonnaise on the gum. Wait a few minutes. Then wipe the gum away and wash your hair as usual.

Pass the mayo, please . . .
Got another good use for mayonnaise? Share it with us at **Almanac4kids.com/tellus.**

SAVE YOUR STUFF!

time capsule, *n.* [1938] 1: a container holding historical records or objects that is deposited for preservation until some future age.

You probably have some pretty special stuff that is important to you: souvenirs, keepsakes, awards, gifts, lucky charms, photos, and the like. Have you ever thought of preserving it in a container, to be opened in 10, 20, or 50 years? You wouldn't be the first!

Ancient Egyptians first used sealed containers to preserve sacred scrolls, statues, and other items. The finest and largest such containers are the pyramids of Egypt.

In 1936, Thornwell Jacobs, the president of Oglethorpe University in Atlanta, Georgia, began the Crypt of Civilization project. (A crypt is a vault or room that is wholly or partially underground.) For the crypt, he remodeled a swimming pool, giving it a 2-foot-thick stone floor, a 7-foot-thick stone roof, and granite walls. The crypt was sealed with a stainless steel door on May 28, 1940. It will not be opened until the year 8113.

These are some of the items in the crypt:

- **1 towel**
- **3 washcloths**
- **1 set of dentures**
- **1 plastic bird**
- **1 piece of aluminum foil**
- **1 golf ball**
- **1 pacifier**
- **1 doughnut cutter**
- **2 ashtrays**
- **1 electric iron**
- **1 toothbrush**
- **1 coat hanger**
- **1 tabletop pinball game**
- **1 fishing rod**
- **1 female mannequin in a glass case**

You can see the crypt's entire inventory at Almanac4kids.com/history.

In 1938, the Westinghouse Electric and Manufacturing Company assembled two identical time capsules. (This was one of the first uses of the term "time capsule.") The capsules were about 7 feet long, shaped like a torpedo, and made of alloyed metal. One had a window so that its contents could be seen and was on display at the 1939–40 New York World's Fair. The other was buried in Flushing Meadows Corona Park in New York City on September 23, 1938, and is marked by a granite monument. It will be opened in the year 6939. Westinghouse buried a second capsule at the site in 1965.

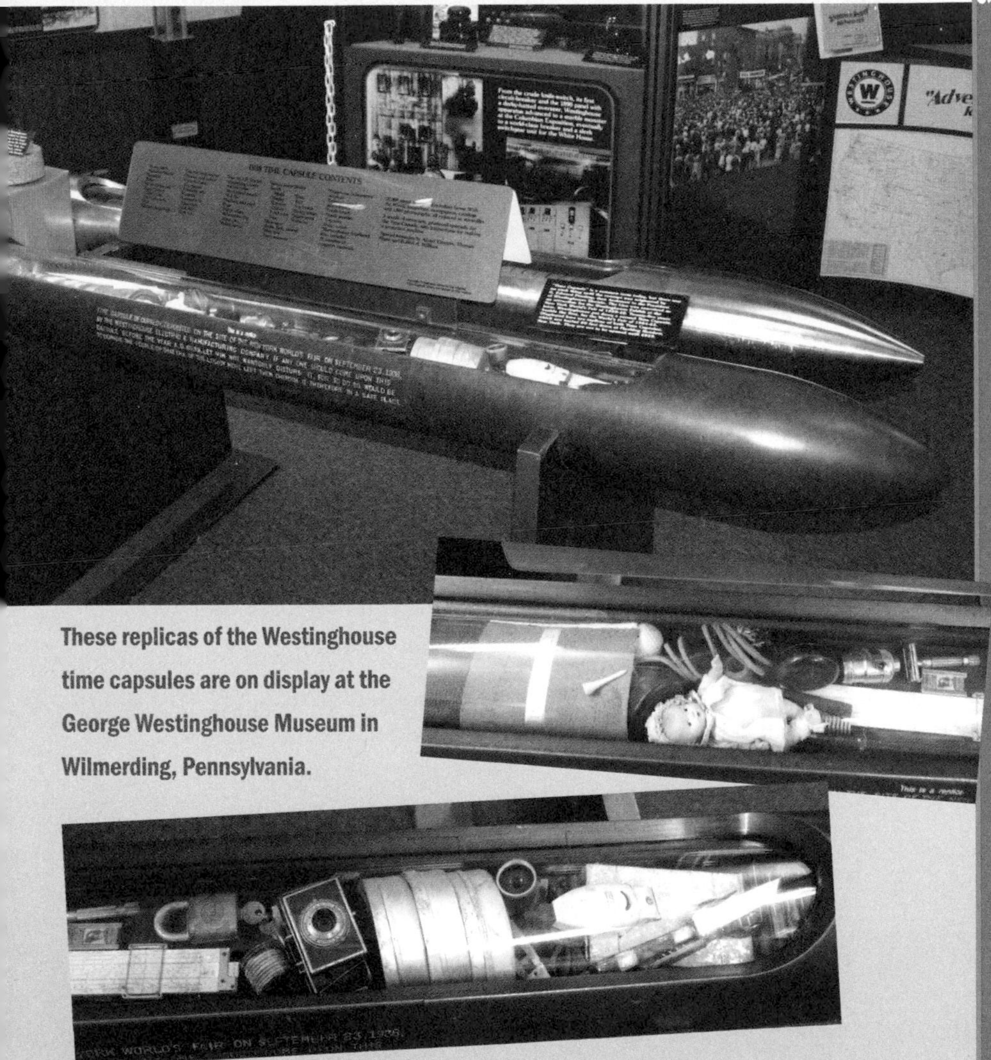

These replicas of the Westinghouse time capsules are on display at the George Westinghouse Museum in Wilmerding, Pennsylvania.

CONTINUED

MAKE A TIME CAPSULE

1. **Set a date for opening.** Choose a birthday or special event but make it no more than 50 years in the future so that you can be fairly certain of being there.

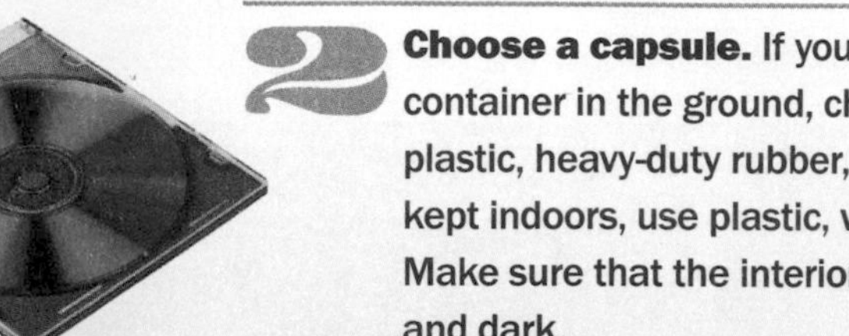

2. **Choose a capsule.** If you plan to bury the container in the ground, choose one made of plastic, heavy-duty rubber, or metal. If it will be kept indoors, use plastic, wood, or metal. Make sure that the interior will stay cool, dry, and dark.

3. **Fill it.** Select personal items and try to have a variety of things: photos, newspaper articles (photocopy the articles to paper; newsprint does not last), advertisements, CDs and DVDs, toys, books, coins, stamps, jewelry, trading cards, and a menu from a favorite restaurant. (No food!) Make a list of the contents. Put items in separate plastic bags to protect them from rubbing against each other.

4. **Have a "sealing" ceremony.** Invite parents and friends. Take photos, including ones of your capsule and its contents. Seal your capsule well.

5. **Store or bury the capsule.** If you do not keepthe capsule where you can see it, write down its location and put that paper in a safe place.

BURIED TREASURES

People at the International Time Capsule Society at Oglethorpe University believe that there are about 10,000 capsules in the world, most of them lost. Don't forget where you put yours!

Where Do You Fit IN YOUR *Family Tree?*

A family tree grows with every generation. Replace the names in this tree with the names of people in your family.

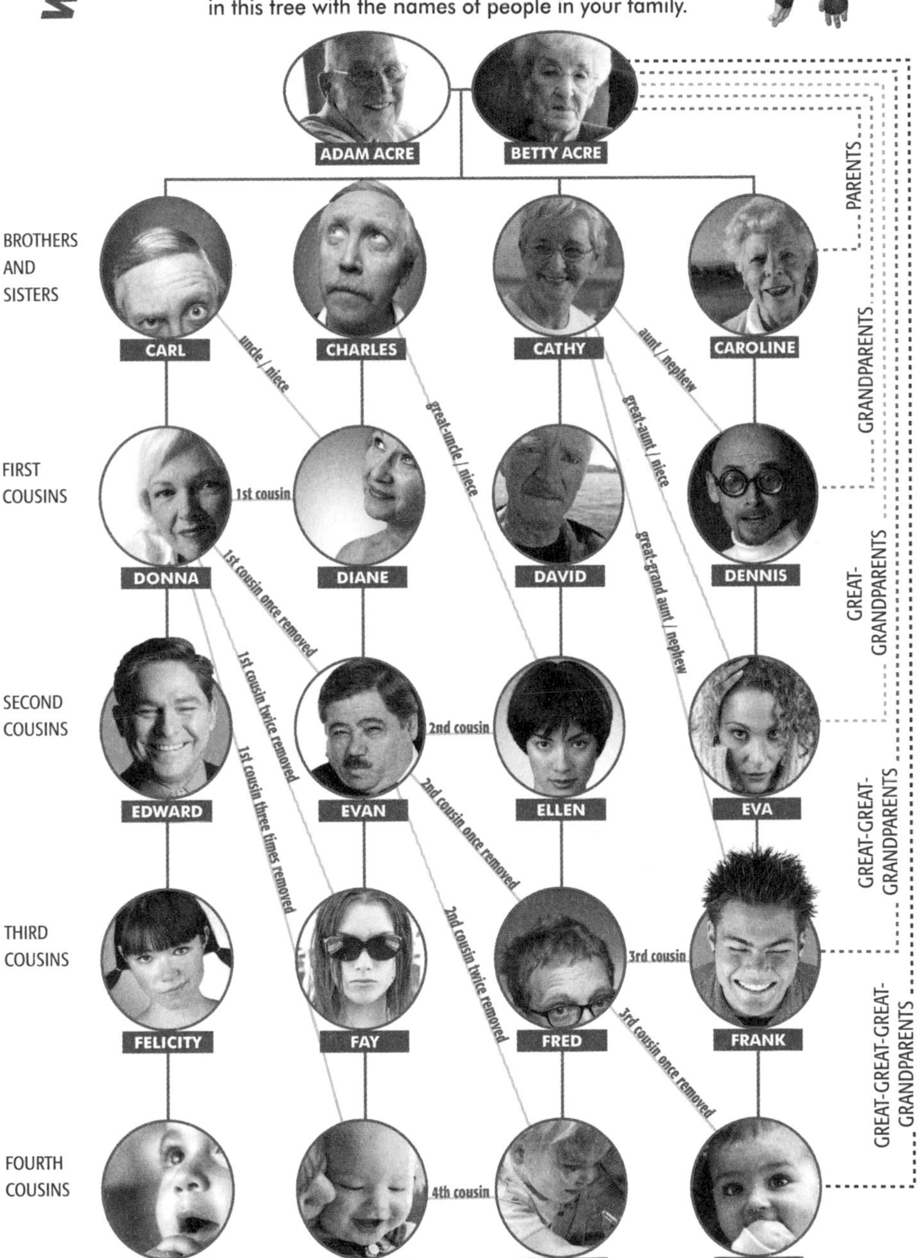

Your Body Rules

Years ago, before the ruler, people created different ways to measure things. Using parts of the body became popular because it was convenient and something everyone could use. Hand-y, huh?

1 inch = the width of a thumb

1 hand = the width of a hand (4 inches)

1 foot = the length of a foot (12 inches)

1 span = the distance between the end of the thumb and the end of the little finger when both are outstretched (9 inches)

1 cubit = the distance between the elbow and the tip of the middle finger (18 inches)

1 yard = the distance from the nose to the fingertip of an outstretched arm (36 inches)

1 pace = one step (2½ to 3 feet)

Measure By Hand

1 foot = 12 thumbs

1 hand = 4 thumbs

1 foot = 3 hands

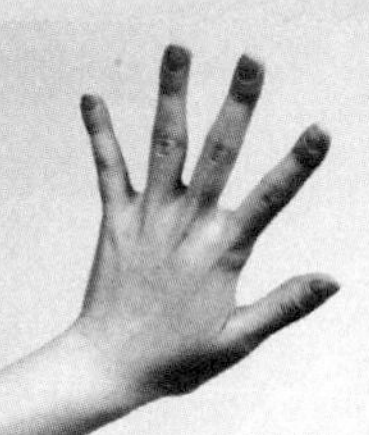

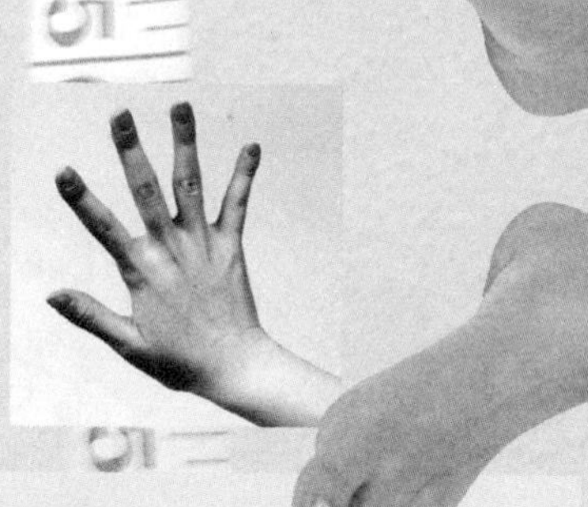

Step Back

The Latin word for "thousand" is *mille,* from which we get our "mile." In ancient Rome, soldiers marched in double-step paces, which measured about 5 feet each. One thousand of these paces equaled 5,000 feet, approximately the 5,280-foot distance that became the modern mile.

TIED UP IN KNOTS

overhand knot

figure-eight knot

granny knot

square knot

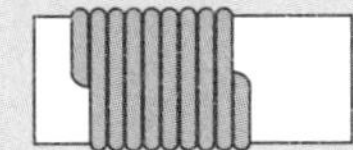
common whipping

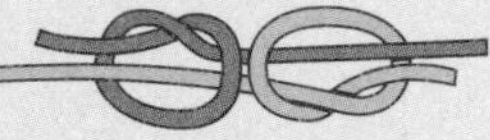
fisherman's knot

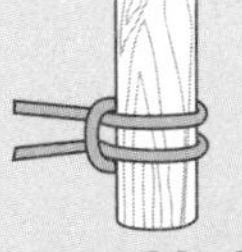
cow hitch

clove hitch

heaving line knot

sheet bend

double sheet bend

sheepshank

bowline

running bowline

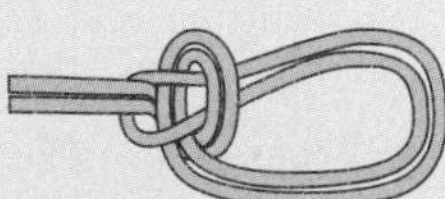
bowline on a bight

Home Cooking

Everyone in the world doesn't eat the same things. To the people in the places below, these foods are delicious!

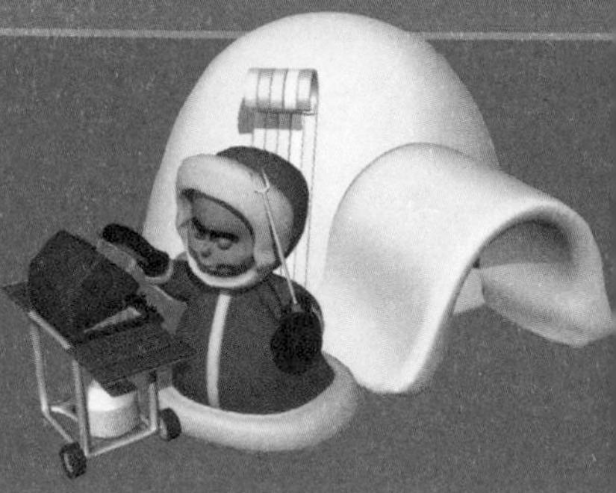

The Arctic:	blubber (raw fat from sea mammals)
Australia:	hamburgers with pickled beets and fried eggs
Brazil:	dried bananas
Chad:	goat meat
China:	deep-fried starfish, sea horses, clam's feet, pigskin jelly
Ecuador:	roasted guinea pig
Egypt:	grilled pigeon
Greenland:	polar bear, narwhal (whale) skin, musk ox stew
Guatemala:	sheep soup
Hong Kong, China:	chicken feet, with or without the bones
Hungary:	scrambled eggs with pig blood
Indonesia:	deep-fried monkey toes, smoked bat meat
Japan:	eel intestines, seaweed, tempeh (pronounced "TEM-pay" and made from moldy soy beans)
Korea:	sea slugs
Mexico:	habaneros (the hottest peppers in the world)
The Netherlands:	raw herring with chopped onions, french fries with mayonnaise
Nicaragua:	sea turtle eggs
Philippines:	fish heads in stews and soups, pig and chicken intestines
Southeast Asia:	durian (a fruit the size of a football that has a hard, spiny shell and yellow, puddinglike flesh inside that smells like gym socks—or worse)
Spain:	fried squid sandwiches
Thailand:	ants, grasshoppers, scorpions
United States:	alligator meat, fried or sautéed frog's legs

HAD ANY FREAKY FOODS? What's the weirdest thing you ever ate? Tell other kids at ALMANAC4KIDS.COM/TELLUS.

ANSWERS TO Mind MANGLERS

PUNNIES

1. Tulips (two lips)
2. A collie-flower
3. Mass-achoo-setts

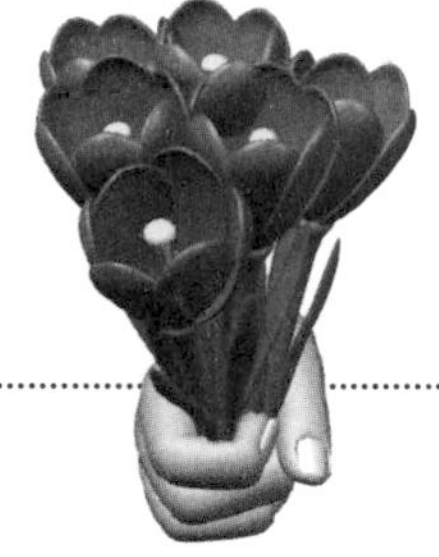

NIFTY NUMBERS

1. When they make 22.
2. None. There is no dirt in a hole.
3. Because then it would be a foot!

SILLY SENSE

1. The half Moon, because the full Moon is twice as light.
2. Because in winter he wears a fur coat and in summer he wears a fur coat and pants.
3. I have my eye on you.
4. Because he tasted funny.
5. You have to be careful not to step in a poodle.

LETTER LOGIC

1. Smiles, because there is a mile between the first and last letters.
2. Enough
3. Drone
4. Madam

Turn to page 133 for the questions

Acknowledgments

PICTURE CREDITS:

ABBREVIATIONS:
ARS—Agricultural Research Service
C—Corbis
GCNY—The Granger Collection, New York
GI—Getty Images
IS—Index Stock
JI—Jupiter Images
NASA—National Aeronautics and Space Administration
NASA/JPL—National Aeronautics and Space Administration/Jet Propulsion Laboratory
NOAA—National Oceanic and Atmospheric Administration
NSSDC—National Space Science Data Center
NWS—National Weather Service
PGC—Pennsylvania Game Commission
SOHO—Solar and Heliospheric Observatory
SS—SuperStock, Inc.
SXC—Stock.xchng
USDA—United States Department of Agriculture

The editors acknowledge IndexOpen.com as the source for numerous images that appear in this publication.

Front cover: (Solar system) Kauko Helavuo/GI. (Horse, Girl blowing bubble) Digital Vision/GI. Other images provided by age fotostock/SS, RubberBall/SS, Stockbyte/GI, Stockbyte/SS, Stockdisc/SS.

Calendar: 17: (Top) Loretta Humble/SXC. 18: (Top) Stockbyte/GI. 20: (Right) Jacob Dingel/PGC Photo. 23: (Center left) Purestock/SS.

Astronomy: 24–25: (Center diagram) NASA/NSSDC/SOHO. 24–25: (Center illustration) Margo Letourneau/David Ziarnowski. 25: (Top right) Purestock/GI. 28: (Center right, both) Rolf Sinclair. (Bottom right) www.knowth.com. 30: Special Collections, Vassar College Libraries. 31: Harvard College Observatory. 32: Lowell Observatory. 33: (Background illustration and inset) NASA. 34: (Inset) NASA/Lunar and Planetary Laboratory. 35: (Top) NASA/JPL-Caltech. 37: (Diagram) David Ziarnowski, based on NASA illustration. 38: (Bottom right) NASA. 39: (Center right) NASA/JPL. 40: (Center left) NASA. 41: Royalty free/C. 42–45: (Illustrations) Carolyn Croll.

Gardening: 46: Sandor Balázs/SXC. 48: (Top left) GI. 52: (Center left) Tom and Margo Letourneau. 53: (Bottom left) Ariel Skelley/GI. 55: (Top left) Indian Harvest Special Foods, Inc. (Center left) Vermont Bean Seed Company. (Bottom left and top right) Seed Savers Exchange. (Bottom right, both) www.tomatobob.com. 56: (Illustration) Renée Quintal Daily. 57: (Bottom right, all) Purdue University. 58: (Center left and top right) W. Atlee Burpee & Co. 60: (Bottom left) RubberBall/JI. 61: (Center right) Lloyd and Susan Bright. 63: Tom and Margo Letourneau.

On the Farm: 65: (Bottom right) Digital Vision/GI. 66: (Top) Cestari, Ltd., Churchville, VA. (Center right) USDA. 67: (Bottom left) Phillip Island Penguin Foundation. 68: (Bottom left) George Doyle/GI. 69: (Top) Bob Burch/IS. 70: (Top right) Stephanie Sanders Ferris. 71: (Top left) www.ncm.org.uk. 73: (Top and center illustrations) Eldon Doty. (Bottom right) Grant Groberg. 75: (Center left) GCNY. 76: (Center left) Stark Bro's Nurseries.

Weather: 78: (Center left) San Diego Historical Society. 79: (Bottom left) Schenectady Museum & Suits-Bueche Planetarium. 81: (Top) Margo Letourneau. (Bottom left) NOAA Photo Library. 82–83: (All) NOAA Photo Library/Historic NWS Collection. 84: (Top illustration) NASA. (Bottom left) NOAA Photo Library/Historic NWS Collection. 85: (Top right, both) NASA/Malin Space Science Systems. (Center right) NASA. 86: 2005 Newsday, Inc. Reprinted with permission. 87: Boston Public Library. 90: (Bottom left) Troy Bartlett. (Top right inset) Jim Morton/Banner Elk Woolly Worm Festival. 91: (Bottom left) E. D. Cashatt/Illinois State Museum.

Nature: 92–93: (Bottom) Yaroos Konkret/SXC. 93: (Top) JI. 94: (Center left) Cameron Raynes/SXC. 96: (Top left) Karen Fenton/SXC. (Center) Colin Joye. (Bottom) Alan Murphy Photography. 97: (Bottom left) Dave Menke/U.S. Fish and Wildlife Service. (Right) Tom and Margo Letourneau. 98: (Top left) the Robot Vegetable/www.middle-fork.org. (Top right) Nick Monaghan/www.lifeunseen.com. 100: (Top left and center right) the Robot Vegetable. (Bottom left) R. Atkinson, University Southern Queensland. (Bottom center) Nick Monaghan. 101: (Center right) Nick Monaghan. 102: (Bottom) Daniel K. Riskin. 103: Digital Vision/SS. 104: Joe Kosack/PGC Photo. 105: (All) © Merlin D. Tuttle, Bat Conservation International. 106: George Grall/GI. 106–107: (Illustrations) Renée Quintal Daily. 107: (Bottom right) Digital Zoo/GI. 108: (Center right) Scott Rheam/PGC Photo. (Bottom) Stephen Lang/Visuals Unlimited. 109: (Top and center left) Jacob Dingel/PGC Photo. (Center right) Brian MacGowan/Purdue University. 111: (Illustrations) Erick Ingraham.

History: 112–113: © Brian A. Vikander/C. 114: (Top right) Roy D. Tea. 115: (Top right) Utah State Historical Society. (Bottom right, both) © 2005, California State Parks. 117: (Bottom) Georgia Department of Archives and History. 118: (Bottom) Georgia Capitol Museum/Office of Secretary of State. 120: (Top left and center right) GCNY. 121: (Center right) National Portrait Gallery, London. 122: (Top right) The Walt Disney Company. 123: (Top) Smokey Bear is the property of the United States, used with permission from the Forest Service, USDA. (Bottom right) Smokey Bear Historical Park. 125: (Top right) The Historical Society of Forest Park, Illinois. (Center left) GCNY. (Bottom center) Charlie Cook. 127: (Center right) Quincy Historical Society. (Bottom left) Tom Grill/C. (Bottom center) Eskimo Pie Collection, National Museum of American History, Behring Center, Smithsonian Institution. 128: (Top center) JI. (Center left, both) Carvel Ice Cream.

Amusement: 137: Blend Images/SS. 138: (Left) GCNY. 140: RubberBall/GI. 142: DAJ/GI.

Sports: 144: (Top) National Portrait Gallery, Smithsonian Institution/Art Resource, NY. 144–145: (Illustration) David Austin Clar. 149: Ciaran Griffin/GI. 151: age fotostock/SS. 152: National Baseball Hall of Fame, Cooperstown, New York. 154: (Top left) Jim Oltersdorf/IS. 154–155: Erwin Bud Nielson/IS. 155: (Center right) Omni Photo Communications Inc./IS. 157: www.lanefrost.com. 158: (Top right and bottom) GCNY. 159: (Bottom left) Lorne Shields. 160: (Top center) GCNY. 161: (Top left) Lorne Shields. (Bottom) GCNY. 162: (Top) NASA. (Bottom left) Sears Historical Archives. (Bottom right) Nautilus, Inc. 163: (Top center) Casey B. Gibson. (Top right) www.sidewaysbike.com.

Health: 164: (Bottom) Dr. David Phillips/GI. 165: (Center left) Purestock/GI. 166: (Top right) Purestock/GI. 167: (Top left) Eric Erbe; digital colorization by Chris Pooley/ARS/USDA. (Top center) Central Microscopy Research Facilities, The University of Iowa, Iowa City, Iowa. 168: (Bottom) Aura/GI. 172: (Center left) Harvard University, Environmental Health & Safety Department. 174: (Bottom) The Smithsonian Institution, Division of Medicine and Science. 174–175: GCNY.

Useful Things: 180: (Bottom) The Archives, Philip Weltner Library, Oglethorpe University. 181: (All) A. John McSweeny; George Westinghouse Museum, Wilmerding, PA. 185: (Illustrations) Margo Letourneau.

CONTRIBUTORS:

Alice Cary: Famous Unknowns, 30–32; Perplexing Pluto, 33; Food Floods, 86–88; The Scoop on Ice Cream, 124–129; Right On, Left-handers, 130–132; Two-Wheeling Through Time, 158–163; You Are Getting Ver-r-r-y Sleepy, 170–173.

Laurie Goldman: Ben Franklin: Statesman . . . Scientist . . . Swimmer?, 144–146.

Mare-Anne Jarvela: Calendar pages, 8–19: Almanac Oddities, 20–23; A Month of Moons, 29; Saturn, the *Real* Lord of the Rings, 34–35; Find My Own Meteorite!, 41; An Earful About Corn, 59; Hey, Ewe!, 64–67; The Color of Money, 119; Mind Manglers, 133; The Game Game, 147; Got Bait?, 148–150; Save Your Stuff!, 180–182; Your Body Rules, 184; Tied Up in Knots, 185.

L. Patricia Kite: The Most Unloved Flower, 46–49; Beans, Bountiful Beans, 52–55; Grow a Vegetable Forest, 56–58; Creepy, Crawly, Coming at You, 98–101.

Stacey Kusterbeck: The Reason for the Seasons, 25–28; Star Art, 42–45; A Prickly Subject, 50–51; Hooray for Horses, 68–72; Ride 'Em, Cowboy!, 154–157; Know Why George Washington Never Smiled?, 174–176 (with thanks to John Martalo); Home Cooking, 186.

Celeste Longacre: Astrology for Pets, 134–135.

Martie Majoros: A Is for Apples, 74–76; Going Batty, 102–105; The Shortcut That Wasn't, 112–115; Jumping for Joy!, 140–143; You Go, Girl!, 152–153.

Sarah Perreault: Make a Dirt Cake, 63; The World's Fuzziest Forecaster, 90–91; Make a Gourd Birdhouse, 96–97; Tracker's Guide, 111; Hocus-Pocus, 136–139; For Crying Out Loud, 168–169; Mayonnaise Magic, 178–179.

Janice Stillman: Dirt, 62; Weather Wizards, 78–81; Beware of Black Blizzards, 82–85; The First Great Gold Rush, 116–119 (with thanks to Deborah Smith).

Heidi Stonehill: 10 Burning Facts About the Sun, 36–40; Whoopee! It's Watermelon Time, 60–62; Fowl Matters, 73; By the Sea, 92–95; Toad-ily Awesome!, 106–107; Meet the Winter Warriors, 108–110 (inspired by the work of biology seminar students of Keene State College, Keene, New Hampshire, under the direction of Professor Susan Whittemore in 2004, and adapted for use courtesy of *The Keene Sentinel,* which published the original work); Three Little Bears, 120–123; In With the Good Air, Out With the Bad, 164–167.

Content not cited here is adapted from *The Old Farmer's Almanac* archives or appears in the public domain. Every effort has been made to correctly attribute all material. If any errors have been unwittingly committed, they will be corrected in a future edition.

Index

A

activities
  catch bait and fish, 148–150
  find a meteorite, 41
  find constellations, 42–45
  fix with mayonnaise, 178–179
  grip a baseball, 151
  grow beans, 52–55
  grow a vegetable forest, 56–57
  grow a square watermelon, 60
  jump rope, 142
  make a Dirt Cake, 63
  make a family tree, 183
  make a gourd birdhouse, 96–97
  make a time capsule, 182
  make a toad abode, 106–107
  make watermelon pops, 61
  perform a card trick, 139
  say tongue twisters, 95
  spit watermelon seeds, 61
  track animals, 111

See the free online Activity Guide at Almanac4kids.com to find more things to do.

air, 167
algae, 94
animal tracks, 111
apples, 74–76
asterism, 43
astrology, for pets, 134–135

B

baseball, 67, 131, 151, 152–153
bats, 102–105
beans, growing 52–54
  varieties, 55
  voting with, 54
bear(s)
  nappers, 108
  Smokey, 122–123
  Teddy's, 120–121
  Winnie-the-Pooh, 121–122
bedbugs, 172
bicycles, history of, 158–163
birds, 51, 96–97, 110
breathing, human, 164–167
bull riding, 154–157

C

cactus, cacti, 50–51
calendar pages, 8–23
card trick, 139
caterpillars, 90–91
Chapman, John (Johnny Appleseed), 75
chipmunk, Eastern, 111
cloud seeding, 81
cold keepers, 109
comet, 30
constellations, 42–45
corn, 59
cows, 65
crying, 168–169
Crypt of Civilization project, 180

D

dandelions, 46–49
desert pack rats, 51
dirt
  Cake, 63
  eating, 62
Dolly, first cloned sheep, 67
Donner Party, 112–115
dreams, 170-171, 173
dust storms, 82–85

E

Earth, 24–25, 34, 38–40, 41
earthquakes, underwater, 93
Egyptians, ancient, 22, 136, 140, 176, 180
equinoxes, 24–26, 28
ewe, 64, 67

F

family tree, 183
fears and phobias, 49, 89
festivals, 26–27
fishing, 148–150
  catching bait, 148–149
food(s)
  floods, 86–88
  of the world, 186
fowl facts, 73
Franklin, Benjamin, 144–146
fruit
  apples, 74–76
  or vegetable?, 77
  watermelon, 60–61

G

Galileo, 34
gardening
  beans, 52–55
  cacti, 50–51
  phobias, 49
  vegetable, 56–57
  watermelons, 60–61
Gehrig, Lou, 152–153
geophagy, 62
Gold Rush, 116–118
grasshoppers, 149
gravity, pull of, 92–93
Greeks, ancient, 32, 38, 54, 136

H

Hatfield, Charles Mallory, 78
hibernation, 108–110
  brown fat, 110
honeybees, 110
horses, 68–72
Houdini, Harry (Ehrich Weiss), 138
huddlers, group, 109

I

ice, 79–80
ice cream, history of, 124–129

J

Johnny Appleseed, 75
jumping rope, 140–143

K

kiteboarding, 146
knots, 185

L

Langmuir, Irving, 79
Leavitt, Henrietta Swan, 31
left-handers, 130–132

M

magic, history of, 136–138
Mars, 32, 85
mayonnaise, uses, 178–179
measurements, with body parts, 184
meteorites, 41
Mitchell, Jackie, 152–153
Mitchell, Maria, 30
money, 119
Moon, 26, 29
  and tides, 92

N

nappers, 108
  and snackers, 109
Native Americans
  Anasazi, 28
  Cherokee nation, 55, 118
  and popcorn, 59

P

penquins, 67
Period-Luminosity Law, 31
pets, 134–135
Phair, Venetia Burney, 32
phobias, 49, 89
planets
  Earth, 24–25, 34, 38–40, 41
  Mars, 32, 85
  Pluto, 32, 33

Saturn, 34–35
Uranus, 34
X, 32
pioneers, 46, 112–115
Pluto, 32, 33
puzzles and riddles, 133
word matches, 57, 147

R

raccoon, common, 111
rain, 78–81
recipes
Dirt Cake, 63
watermelon pops, 61
Red Rock (bull), 157
Robert-Houdin, Jean Eugene, 138
rodeos, 154–157
Romans, ancient, 27, 54, 74, 124, 136, 176
Roosevelt, Franklin D., 128
Roosevelt, Theodore "Teddy," 120–121, 142
Ruth, Babe, 152–153

S

Saturn, 34–35
sea creatures, 94–95
seasons, 24–28
seaweed, 93–94
sheep, 64–67
sleep, 170–173
and dreams, 171–173
solstices, 24–25, 27
spiders, 98–101
squirrel, red 111
stars, 42–45
brightness and distance of, 31
in constellations, 42–45
Stonehenge, 27
Sun, 36–40
and seasons, 24–28
shines on the Moon, 29
spots, 40
swimming, 144–146

T

tears, 168–169
teeth, 174–176
Thomas, Robert B., founder of *The Old Farmer's Almanac,* 3
time capsules, 180–182
toads, 106–107
Tracker's Guide, 111
tsunamis, 93

V

vegetable(s)
corn, 59
varieties, 57–58
or fruit?, 77

W

warts, 177
Washington, George, 174–176
watermelon, 60–61
weather
cloud seeding, 81
dust storms, 82–85
and food floods, 86–88
makers, 78–80
phobias, 89
proverbs, 91
rain, 78–81
wind on sea, 92
wool, 66–67
woolly bear (caterpillar), 90–91
worms, 148
wren, cactus, 51

Z

zodiac, signs of, and pets, 134–135